dialogues: irena haiduk + martine syms

For the ICA's *Dialogues* series, two curators invite two artists to each create an independent project that activates the distinctive "V" shape of its second floor galleries. The conversation continues in the related publication series. Each artist determines the contents of their half of the publication, which also includes texts from each curator. Dialogue through and about distinct artistic visions unfolds in the spaces of both the gallery and publication, revealing overlap, resonance, and difference.

For the inaugural installment, artists Irena Haiduk and Martine Syms created new works developed for the ICA. Both are committed to ongoing research-based projects that reshape familiar entities, such as the corporation or the personal digital assistant, into complex works of art. These multi-disciplinary projects are not merely representations of those things, but are the things themselves: a corporation founded by Haiduk and a chatbot coded by Syms. Marked by each artist's visual style and conceptual approach, these projects inhabited the ICA as interactive platforms that invited participation.

By reinventing familiar commercial and technological forms, the artists offer calls to action. They ask us to rethink our relationships to things and to others, and to shift how we engage with dominant structures. Each of these projects is a chapter within a larger work that will continue to evolve over time.

BETHANY ALLEN
SAMANTHA BEST
NORA BUTKOVICH
MADISON HALL
ANDY CLIFFORD
NICK CRIDER
CIELLE DULLAS
IRENA HAIDUK
NICOLE KILLIAN
DYLAN LANGUELL
MARGO LENTZ-MEYER
LIN QIAN
RICARDO VICENTE JOSE RUIZ
SHELBY SCHALES
SYD SCOTT
MJ SEQUEIRA
ANNA SHTEYNSHLEYGER
PAUL SMITH
EGBERT VONGMALAITHONG

TABLEAU ÉCONOMIQUE

THINGS CANNOT
BE BOUGHT.

THOSE WHO THINK
THINGS CAN
BE BOUGHT THINK
PEOPLE CAN
BE BOUGHT TOO.

THE WILL TO POSSESS
IS THE COLONIAL
ADMINISTRATION OF
ALL LIFE:

TURNING PEOPLE INTO
THINGS AND
THINGS INTO PEOPLE

(AS IF THE TWO WERE
DIFFERENT).

THERE IS NO
DIFFERENCE BETWEEN
PEOPLE AND THINGS.

THERE IS ONLY
SOLIDARITY BETWEEN
THEM.

THE WAY YOU
TREAT ONE IS THE
WAY YOU
TREAT THE OTHER.

YOU CAN'T BUY
EITHER.

MONEY’S HOLD ON
THINGS
IS PROVISIONAL.

ONLY LOVE CAN BIND
THINGS TOGETHER.

THINGS CANNOT BE POSSESSED.

FOR FIVE HUNDRED
YEARS,
THE ENLIGHTENED
WILL MADE
IMAGES, DESIRES AND
ECONOMIES.

UNDER THIS ADMINISTRATION, OUR GREATEST RIGHTS ARE TO POSSESS AND CONSUME.

CONSUMING THINGS
LIKE THIS MAKES
EVERYTHING TRASH.

WE DISPOSE THE
WORLD.

SOON THERE WILL BE
NO WORLD TO
PHYSICALLY INHABIT.
OUR IMAGES WILL
BE ALL WE HAVE LEFT,
AND OUR GIANT,
BODILESS EYES.

IN THE END, ALL
IMAGES WE MADE ARE
THE CATALOG OF
WHAT WE ANNIHILATED.

OURSELVES INCLUDED.

HOW DO WE MAKE
IMAGES THAT DO NOT
DELETE THE WORLD?

HOW DO WE SURROUND
OURSELVES
WITH THINGS IN THE
RIGHT WAY?

THIS IS THE TASK OF EXHIBITION.

OUR ART INSTITUTIONS
“CARE” FOR THINGS.

THEY COLLECT,
STORE,
ARCHIVE, EMBALM,
DUST, POLISH,
CLIMATE CONTROL,
HYGIENIZE,
STERILIZE.

THEY THINK:

THAT THINGS CAN BE
POSSESSED THIS WAY,

THAT MAKING HISTORY
IS HOLDING ONTO TIME,

THAT THINGS CAN BE
PRESERVED.

THAT HEAVEN ONLY
ADMITS THE DEAD.

LIVING THINGS PLAY
DEAD IN
GRAVEYARDS TO
HIDE.
WHO WOULDN'T?

BEING SURROUNDED
BY
CORPSES IS SCARY.

ART REQUIRES CONTACT.

THIS CONTACT IS AN
ECONOMY
OF MAKING AND
FEELING.

EXHIBITION IS A
DEMONSTRATION OF
ECONOMY.

DAIMON, DAEMON,
DEMO, DEMON,
DEMOS, MONERE,
MONSTRUM,
MONSTER.

DEMONSTRATE.

ECONOMY IS WITHIN
US.
IT IS NOT THE WEATHER.

ECONOMY IS OUR
HOME,
WHERE WE WORK.

WORK CAN'T BE
BOUGHT.

YOU CAN'T PAY FOR LOVE.

TO BECOME A TRUE
INFRASTRUCTURE,
THE ART INSTITUTION
CAN NO LONGER
POSSESS.

TO LEARN SOMETHING
ABOUT ITSELF,
IT MUST GIVE UP CONTROL
AND LET ANOTHER
ENTER AND POSSESS IT.

A DEMON.

AN ECONOMY.

WE MUST LEARN HOW
TO STOP WANTING
WHAT WE WANT, AND
LET THE DEMON
WORK THROUGH ALL
OUR PARTS.

IT SINGS:

TO GIVE POWER IS TO
GIVE UP POWER.

TO GIVE POWER IS TO
GIVE UP POWER.

TO GIVE POWER IS TO
GIVE UP POWER.

TO GIVE POWER IS TO
GIVE UP POWER.

TO GIVE POWER IS TO
GIVE UP POWER.

TO GIVE POWER IS TO
GIVE UP POWER.

TO GIVE POWER IS TO
GIVE UP POWER.

TO GIVE POWER IS TO
GIVE UP POWER.

WE NEED A PLACE THAT
MAKES LIVING.

AN ECONOMY WHERE
WHAT BINDS IS LOVE.

THIS SHOULD COME
NATURALLY TO ART.

BEAUTY LOVES US.

THIS LOVE IS IN OUR SKIN.

TIME IS NOT THE ENEMY.

IT IS AN ARRANGEMENT
OF LIVING.

IRENA HAIDUK
2019

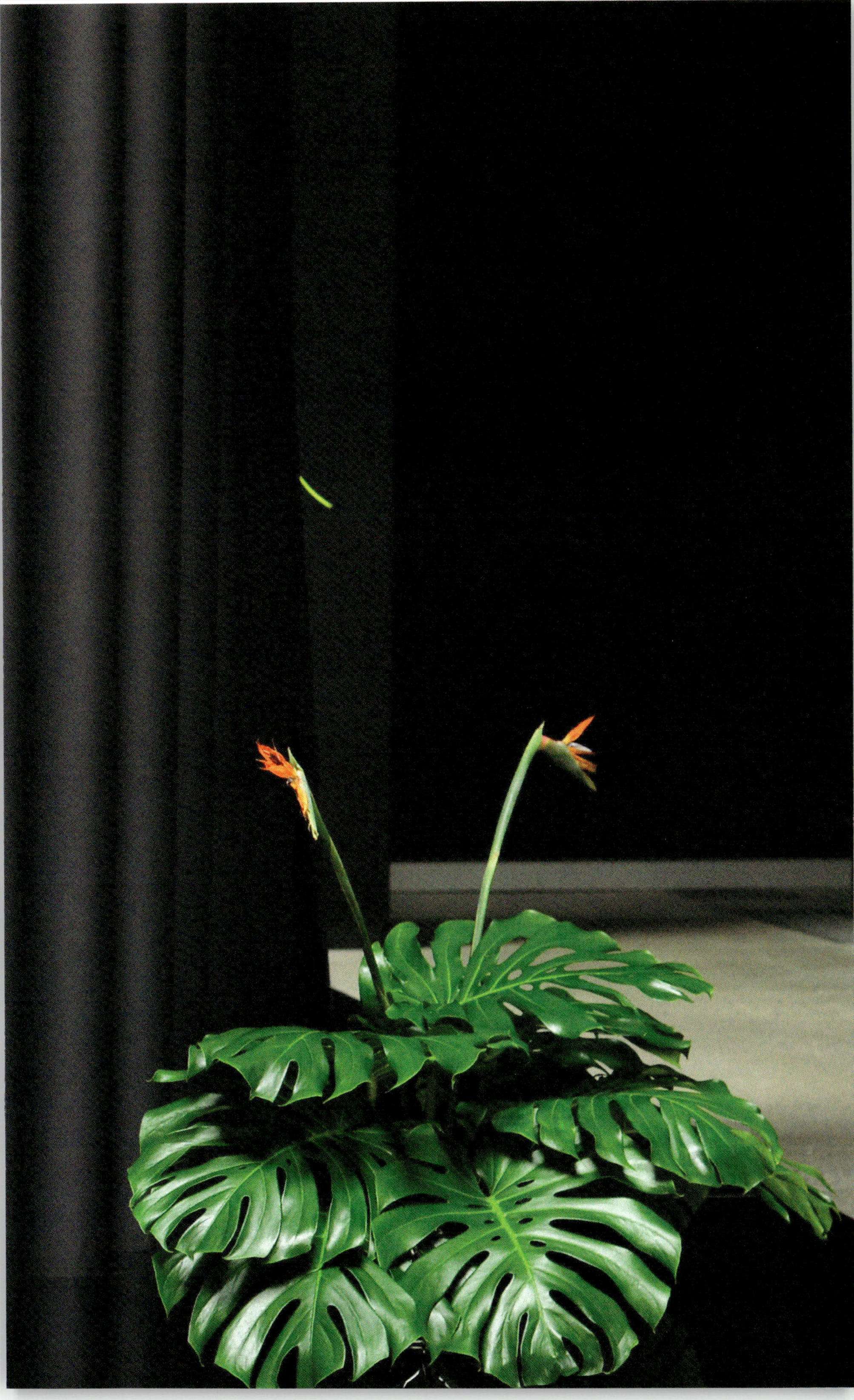

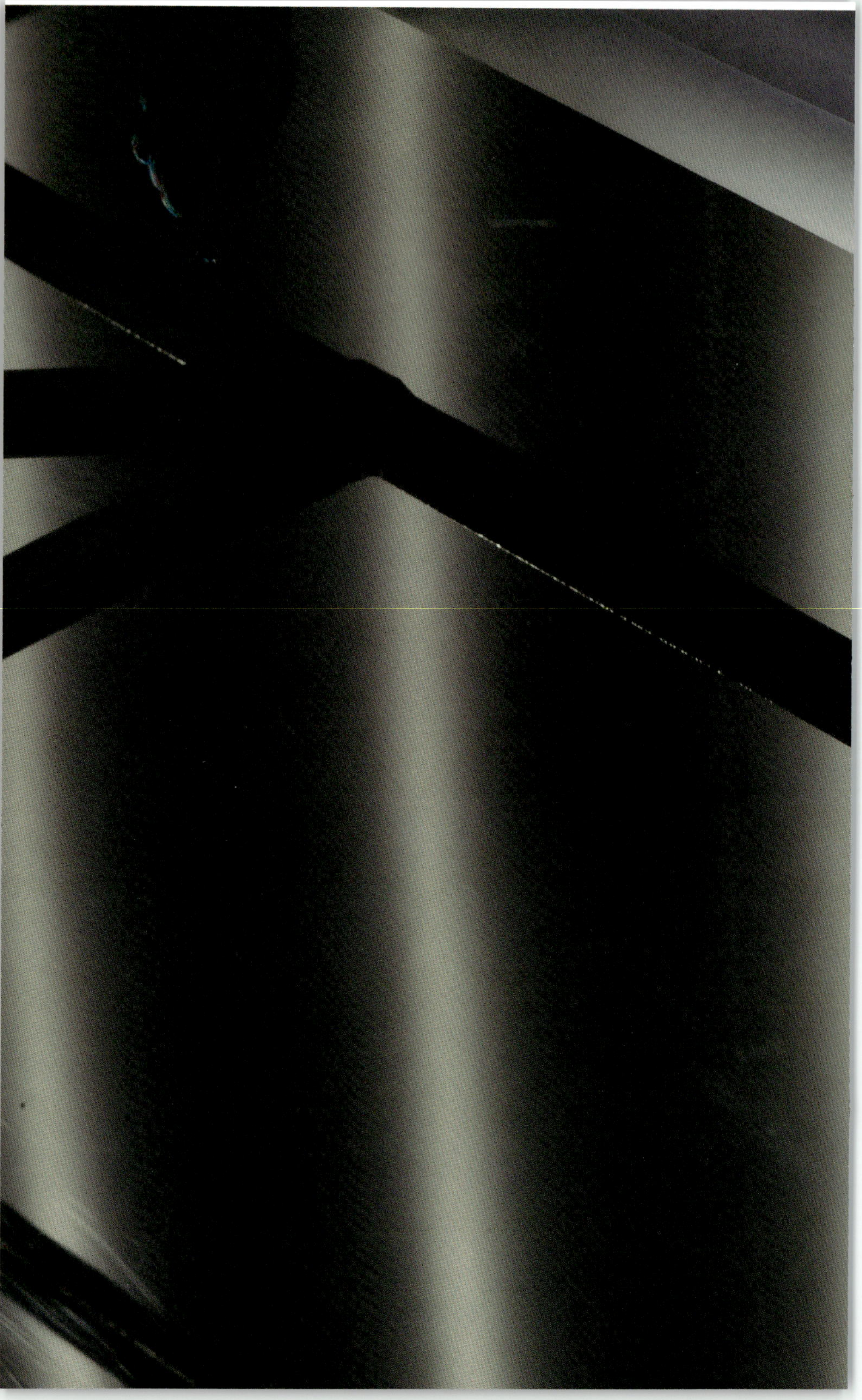

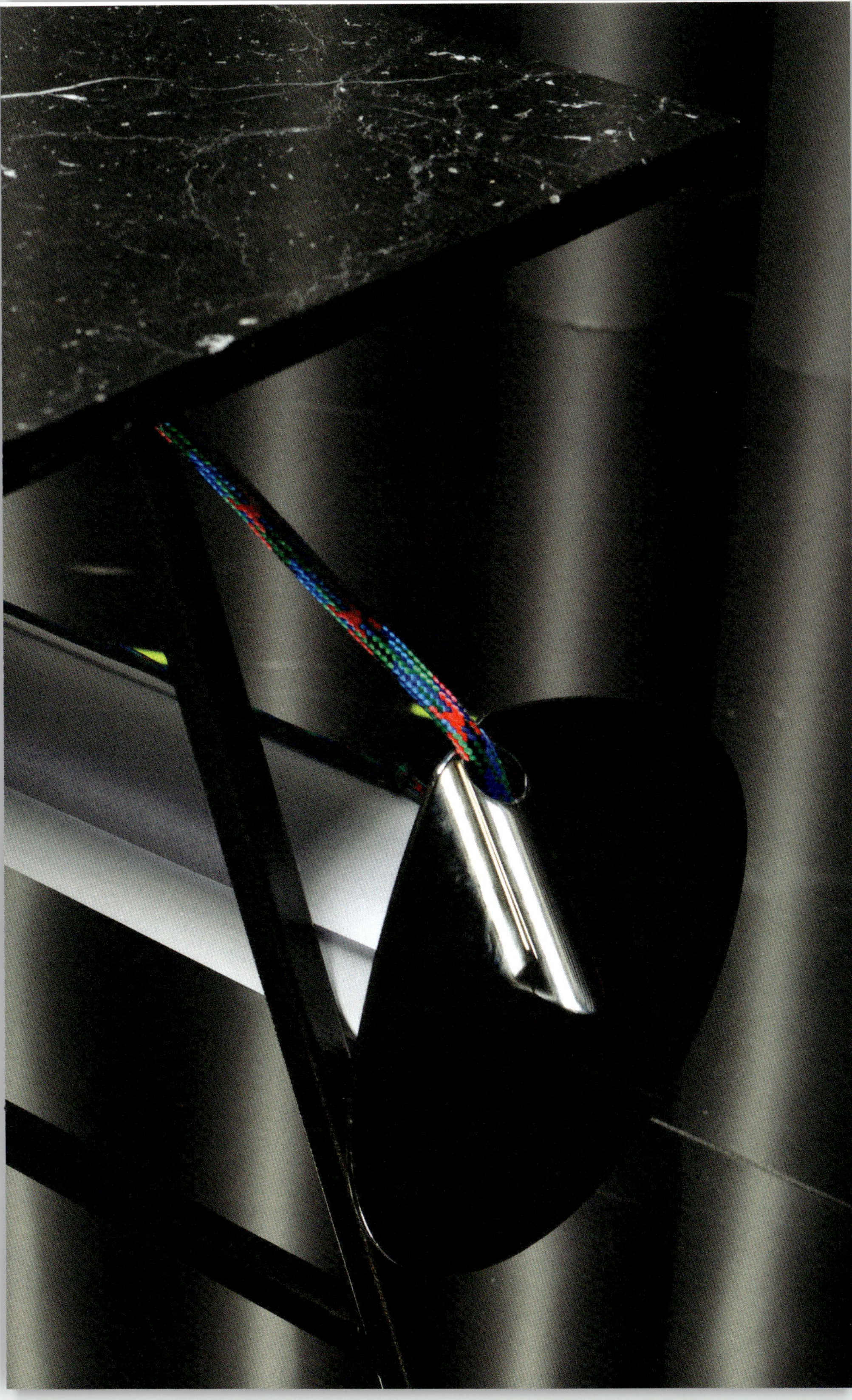

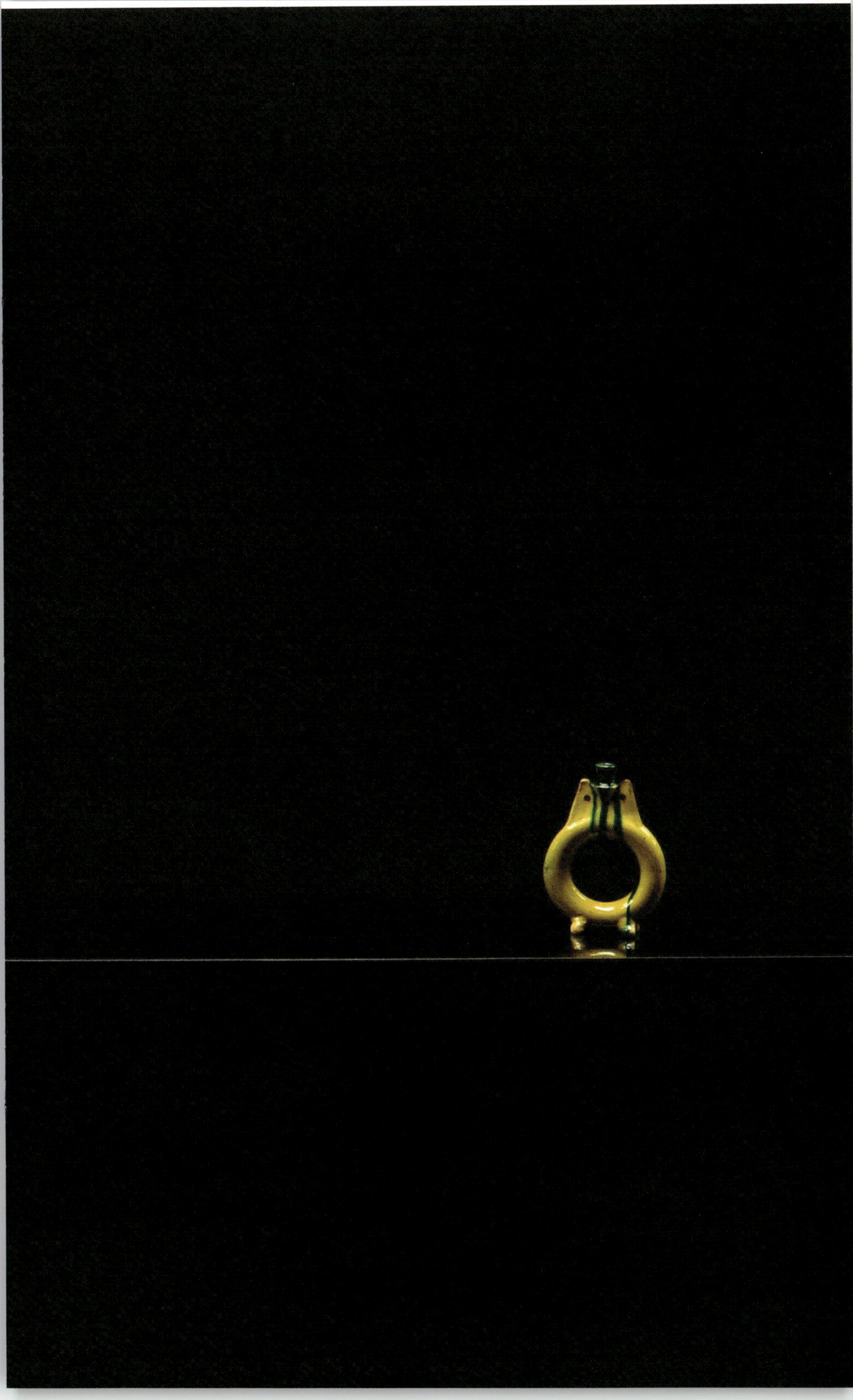

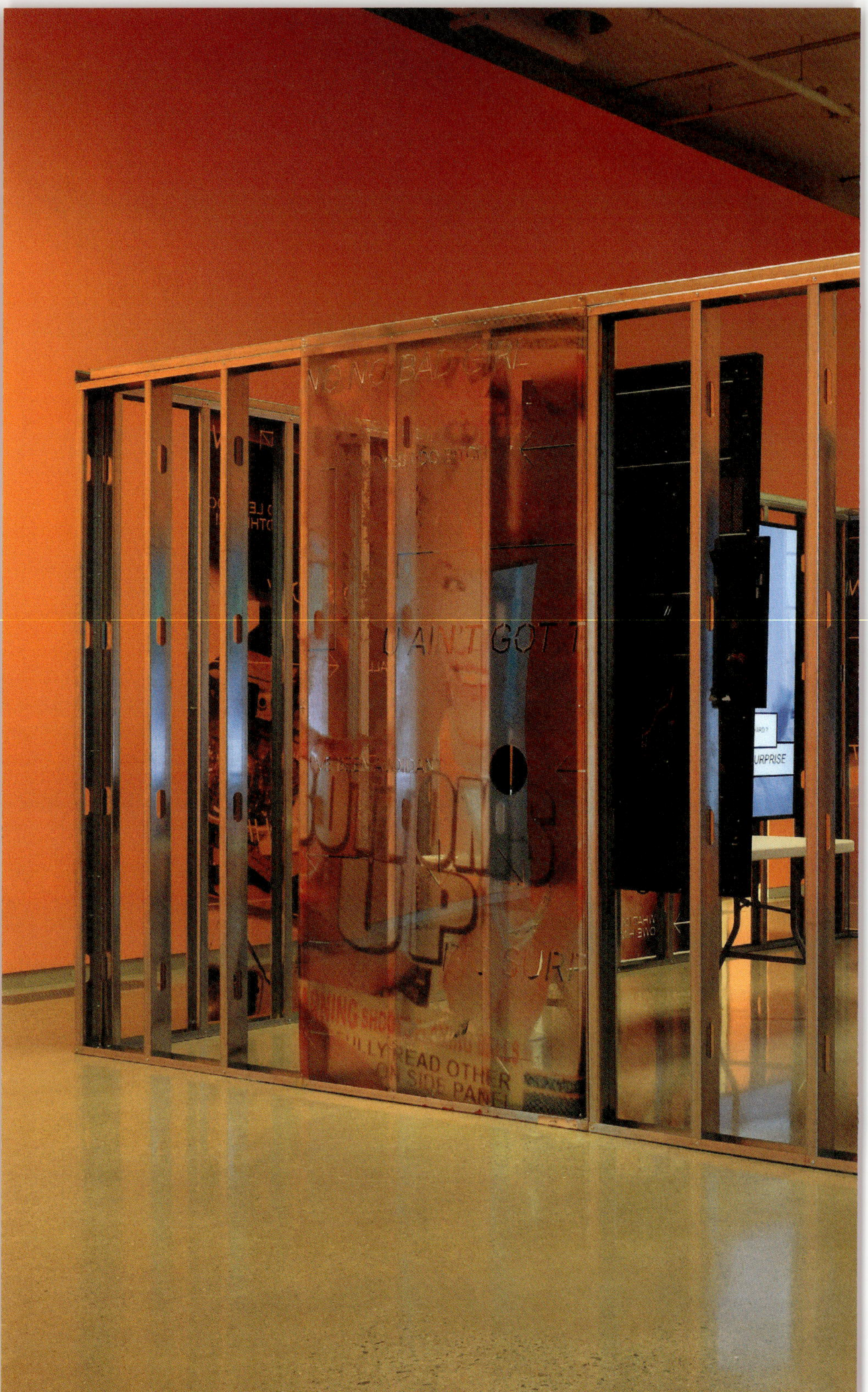
U AIN'T GOT T
URPRISE
READ OTHER
ON SIDE PANEL

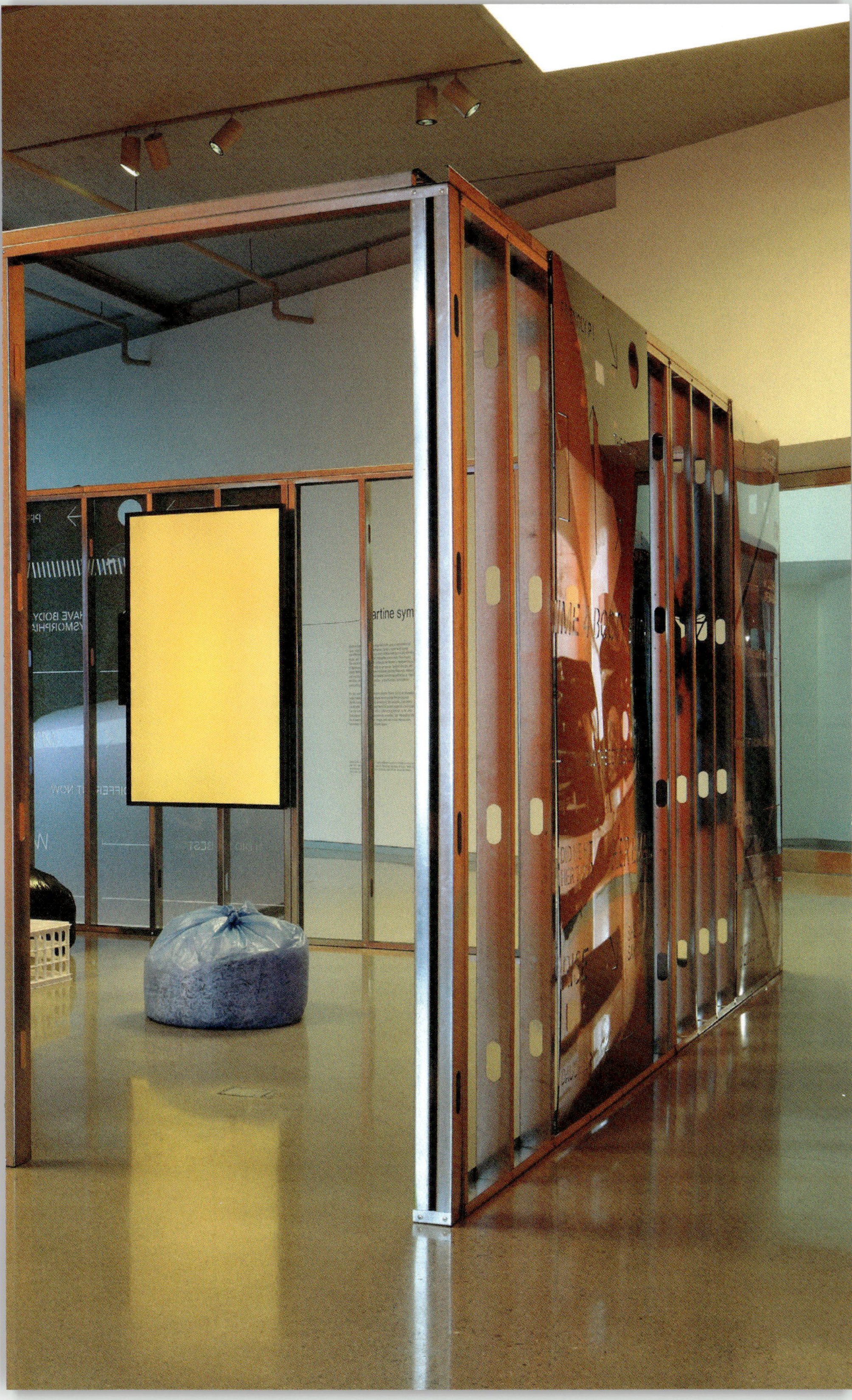

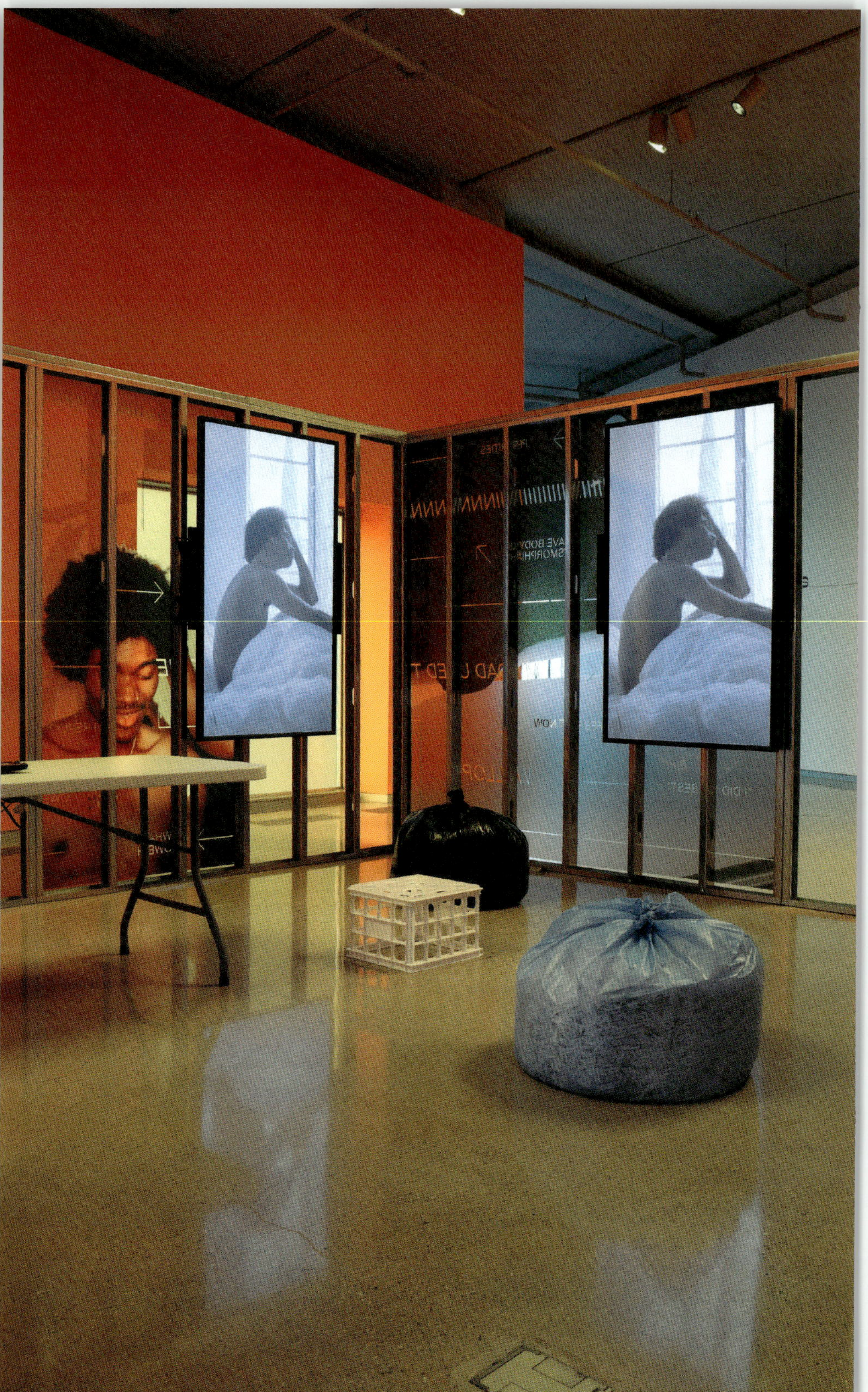

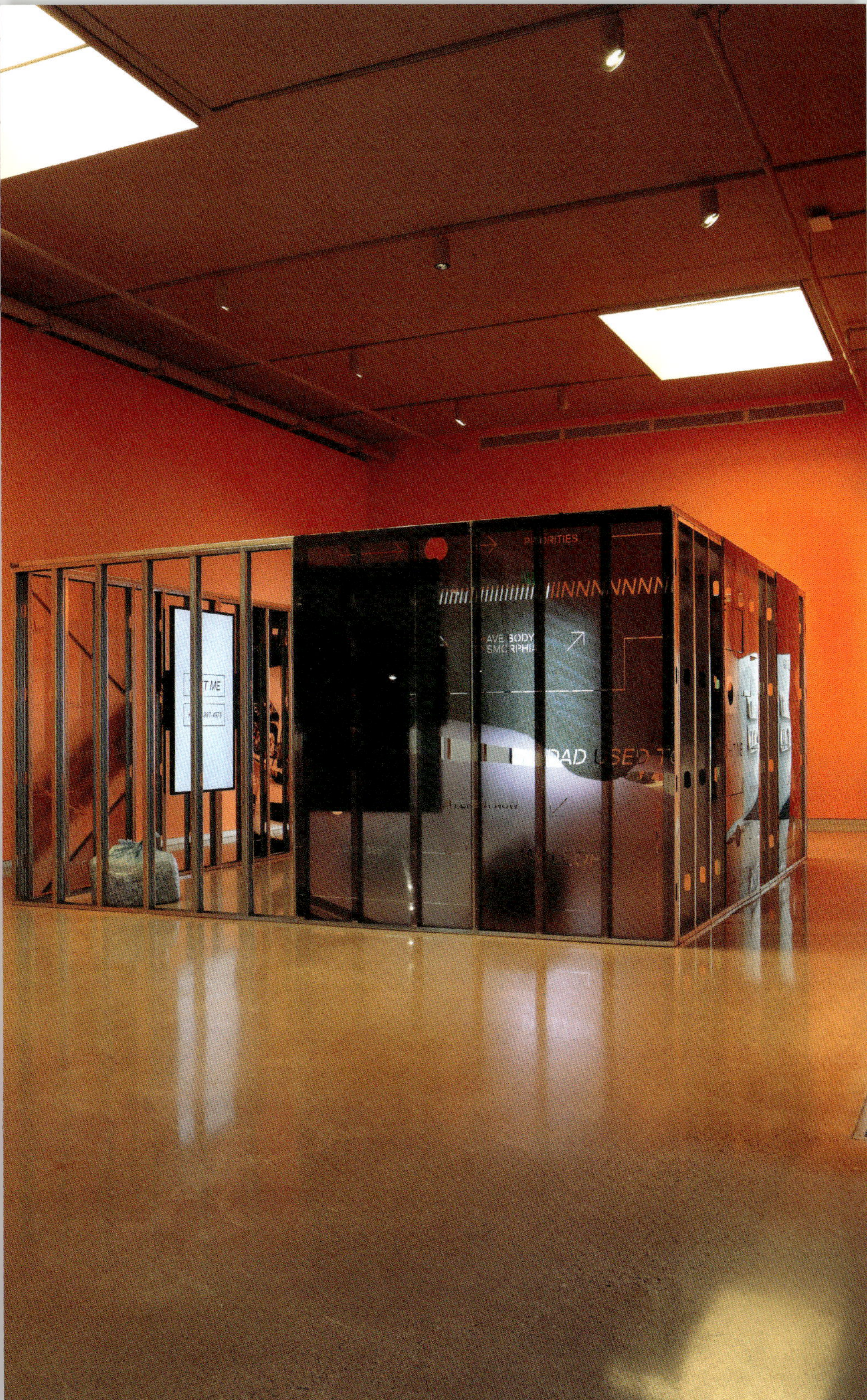
PRIORITIES

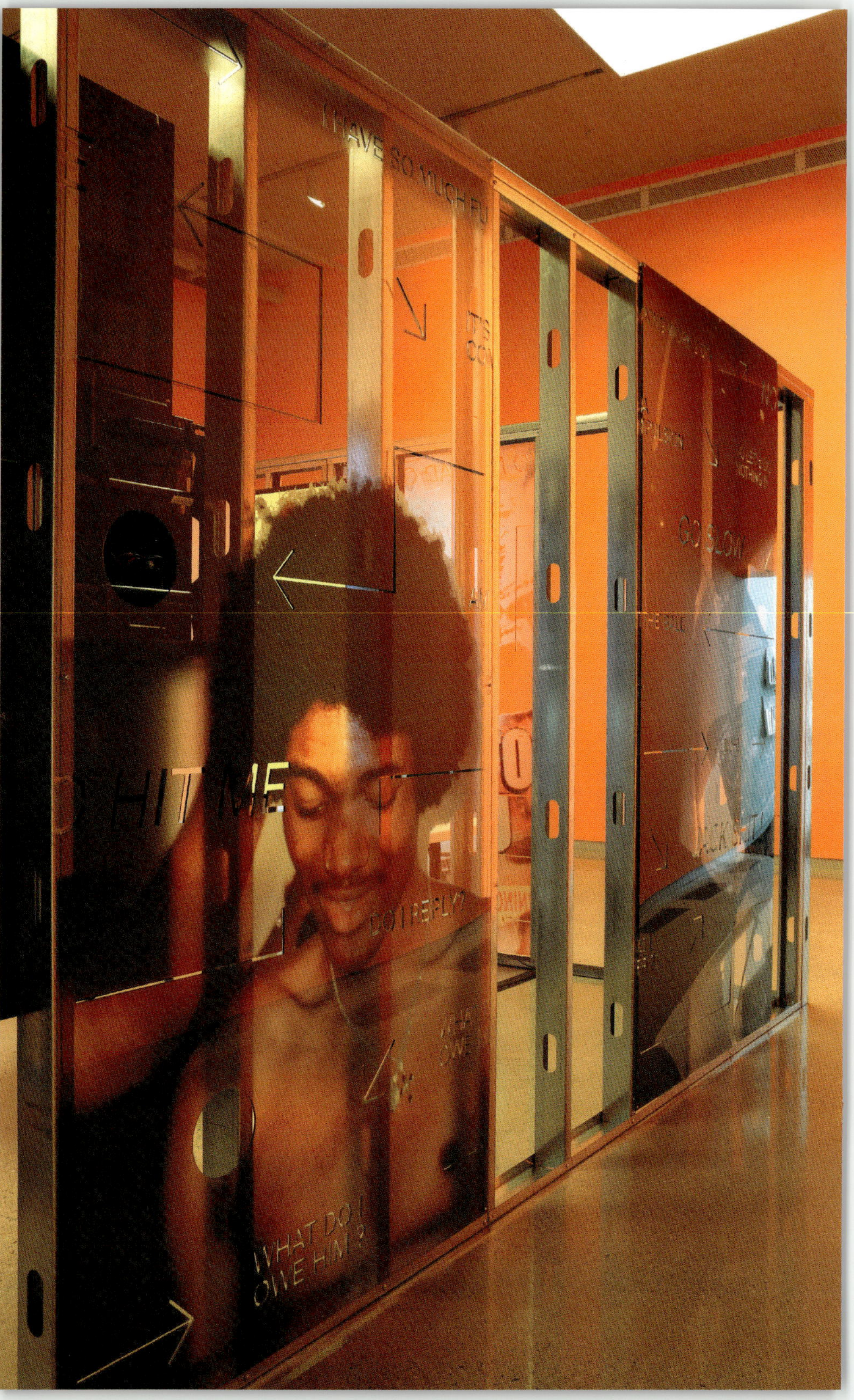
I HAVE SO MUCH FU
GO SLOW
HIT ME
WHAT DO I
OWE HIM ?

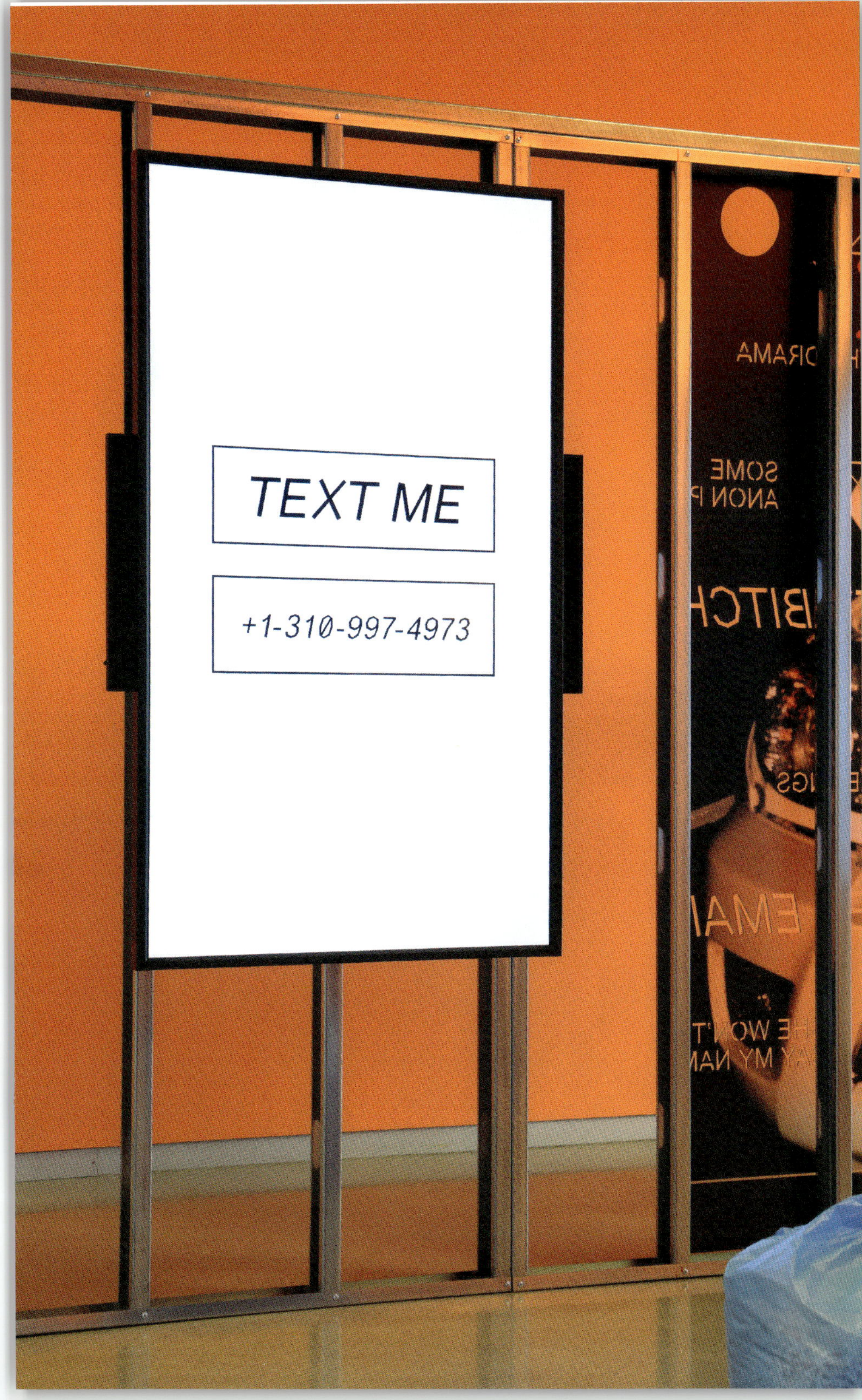
TEXT ME
+1-310-997-4973

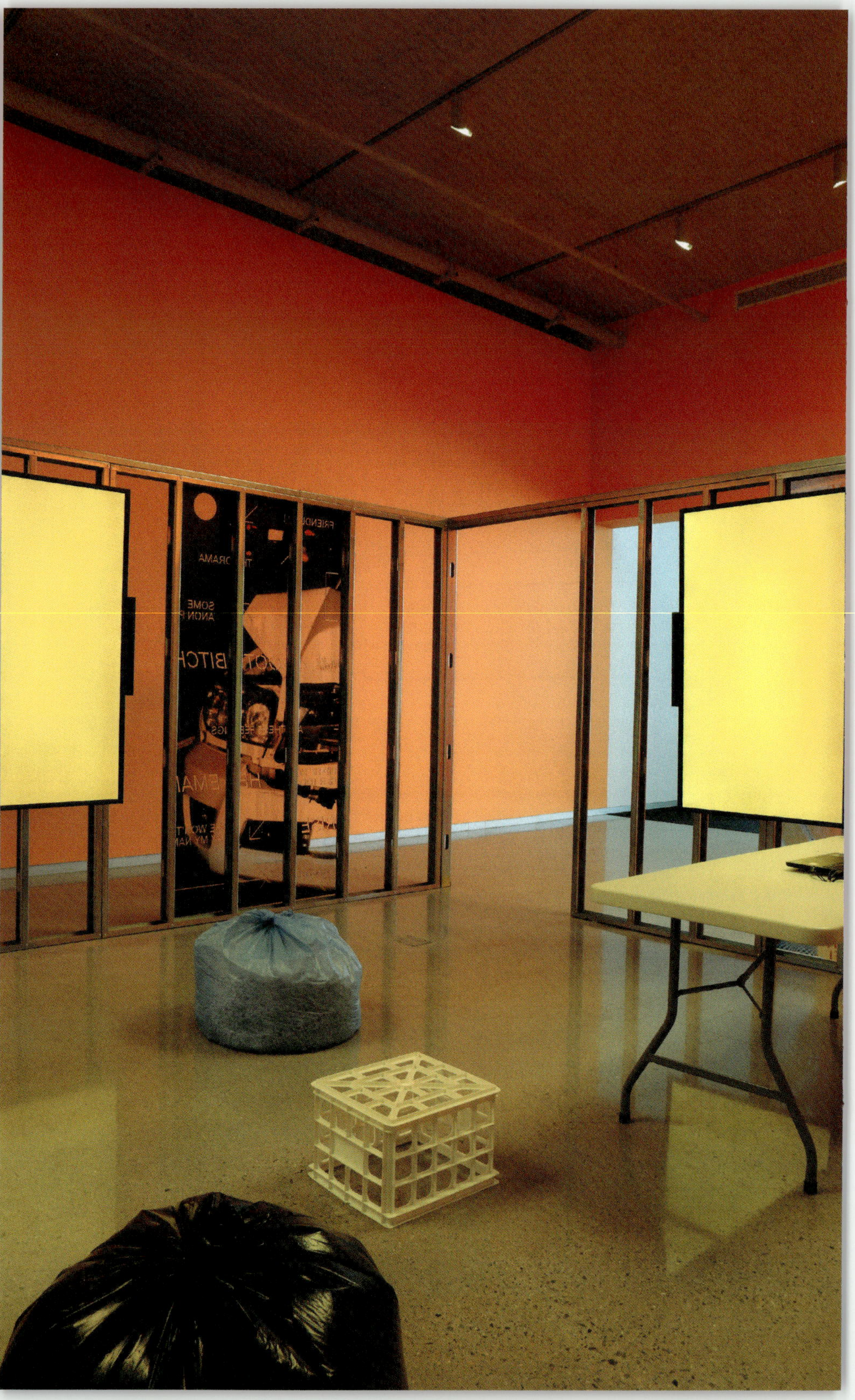

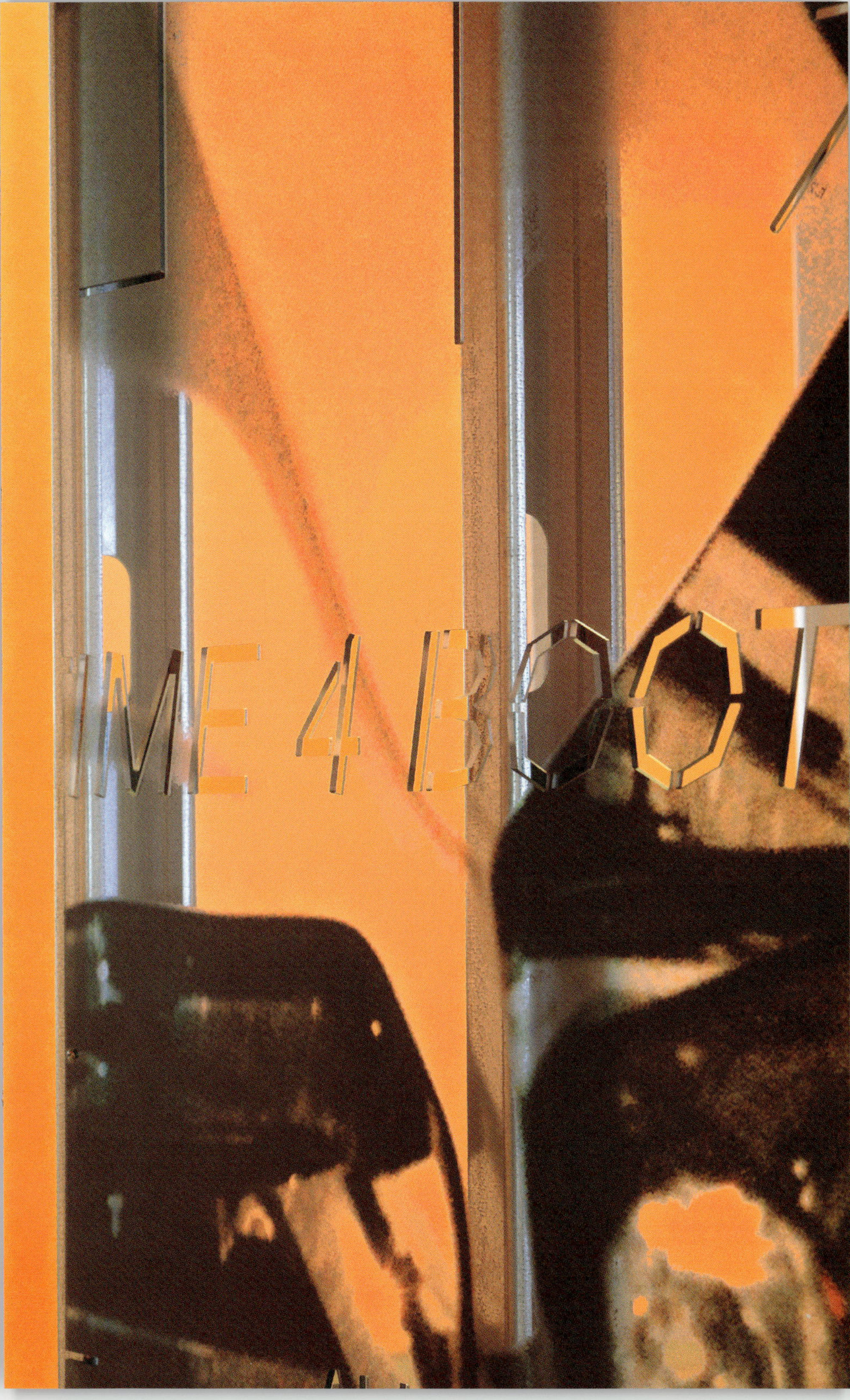
IME 4 BOOT

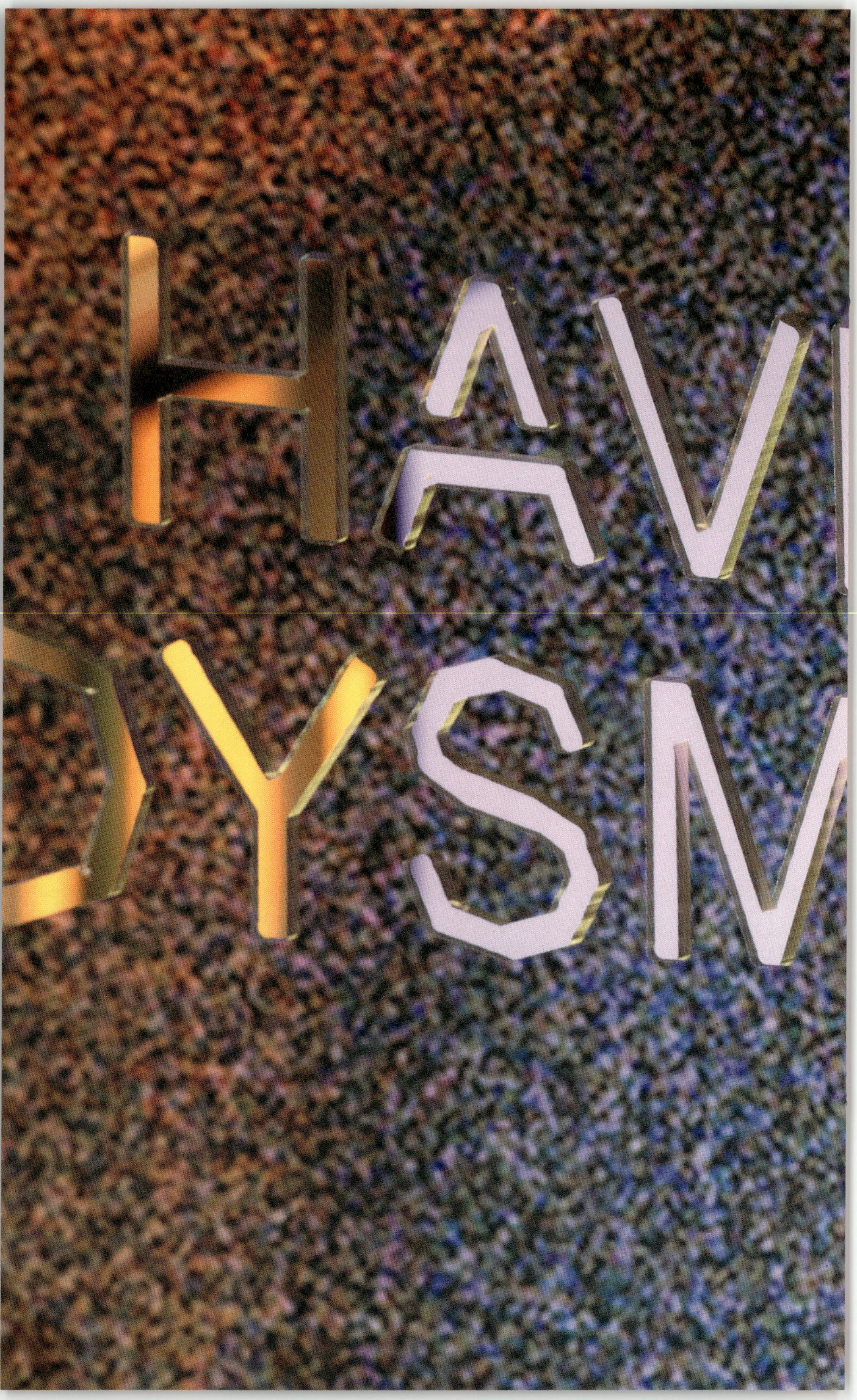

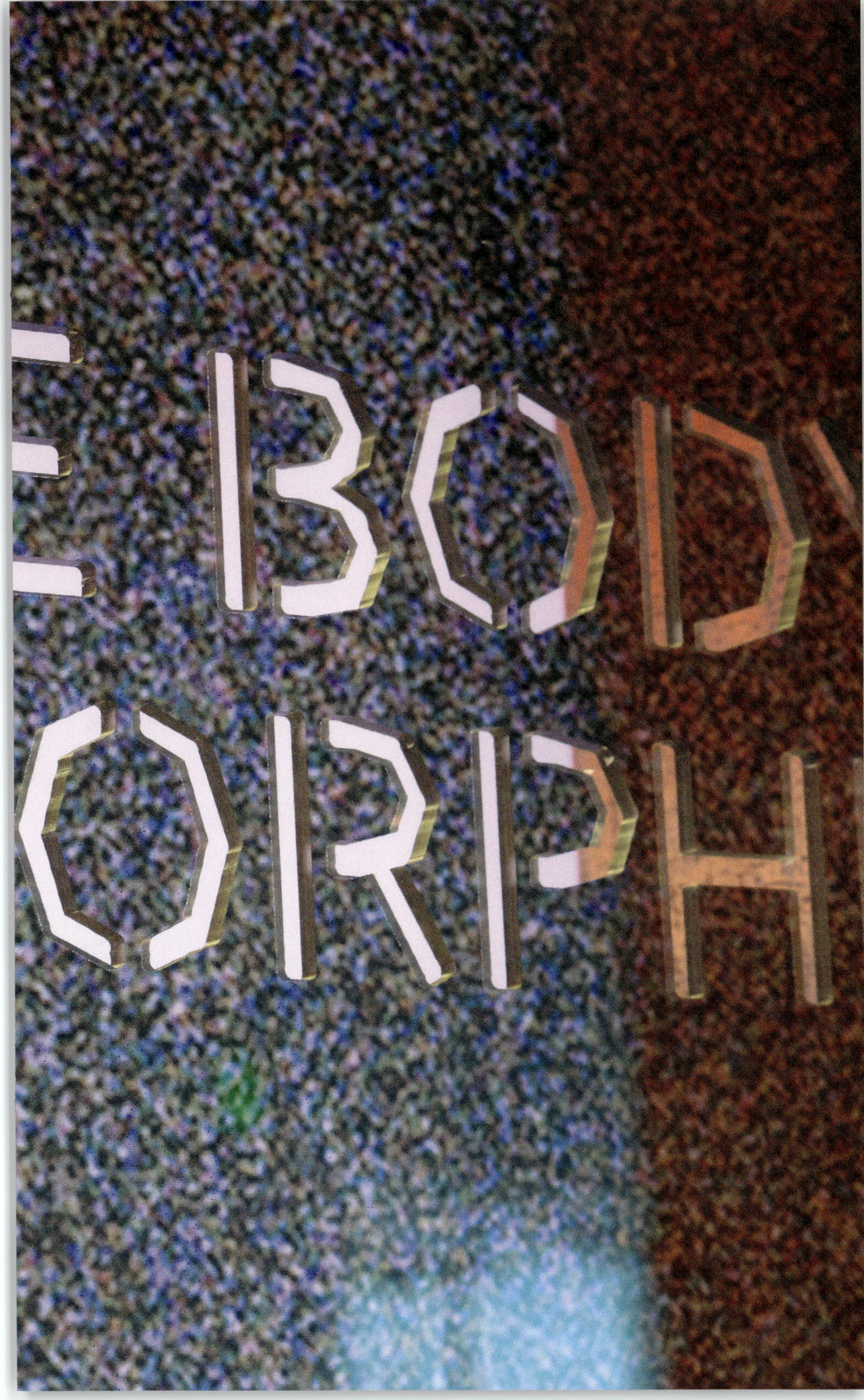

MARTINE SYMS

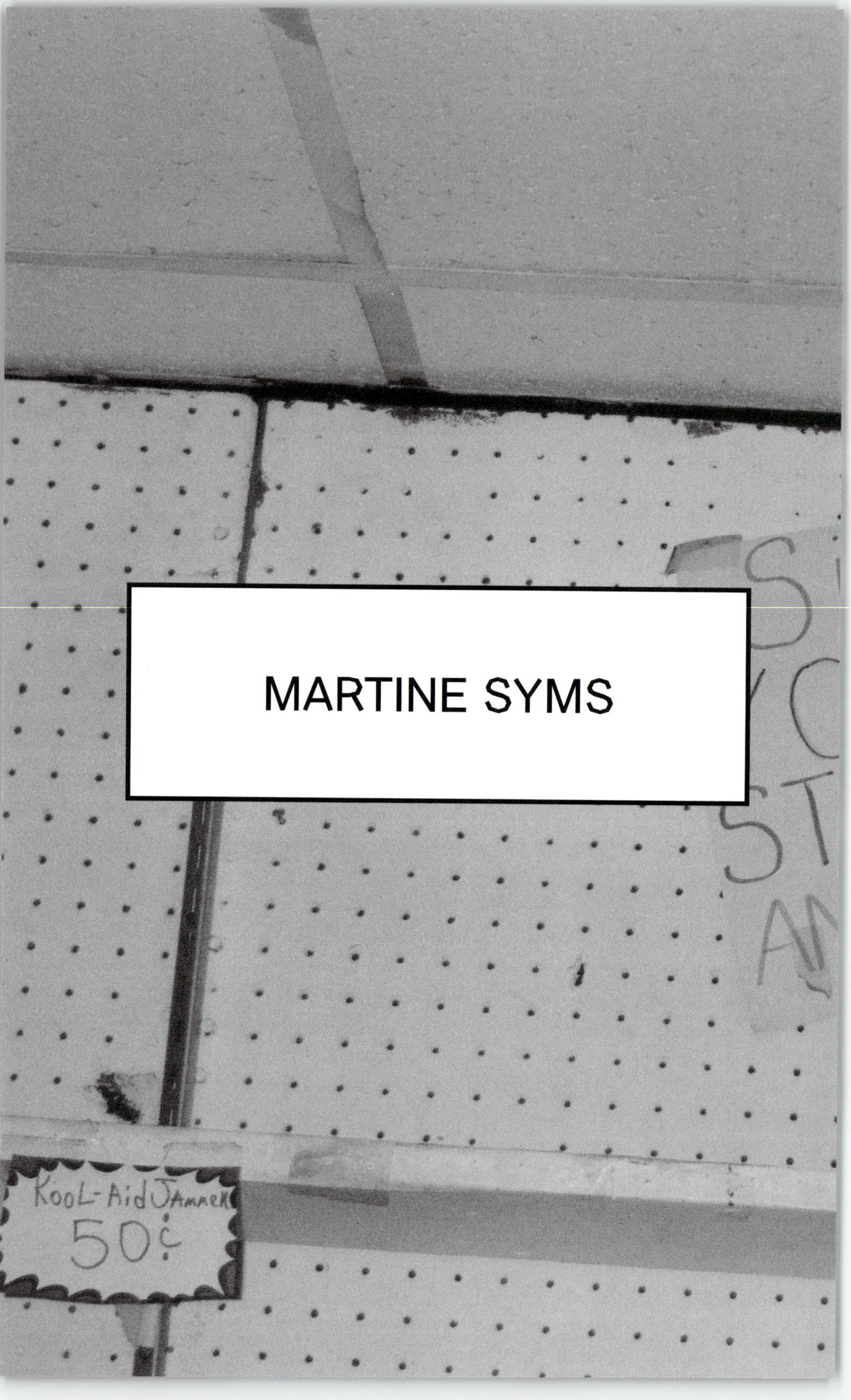

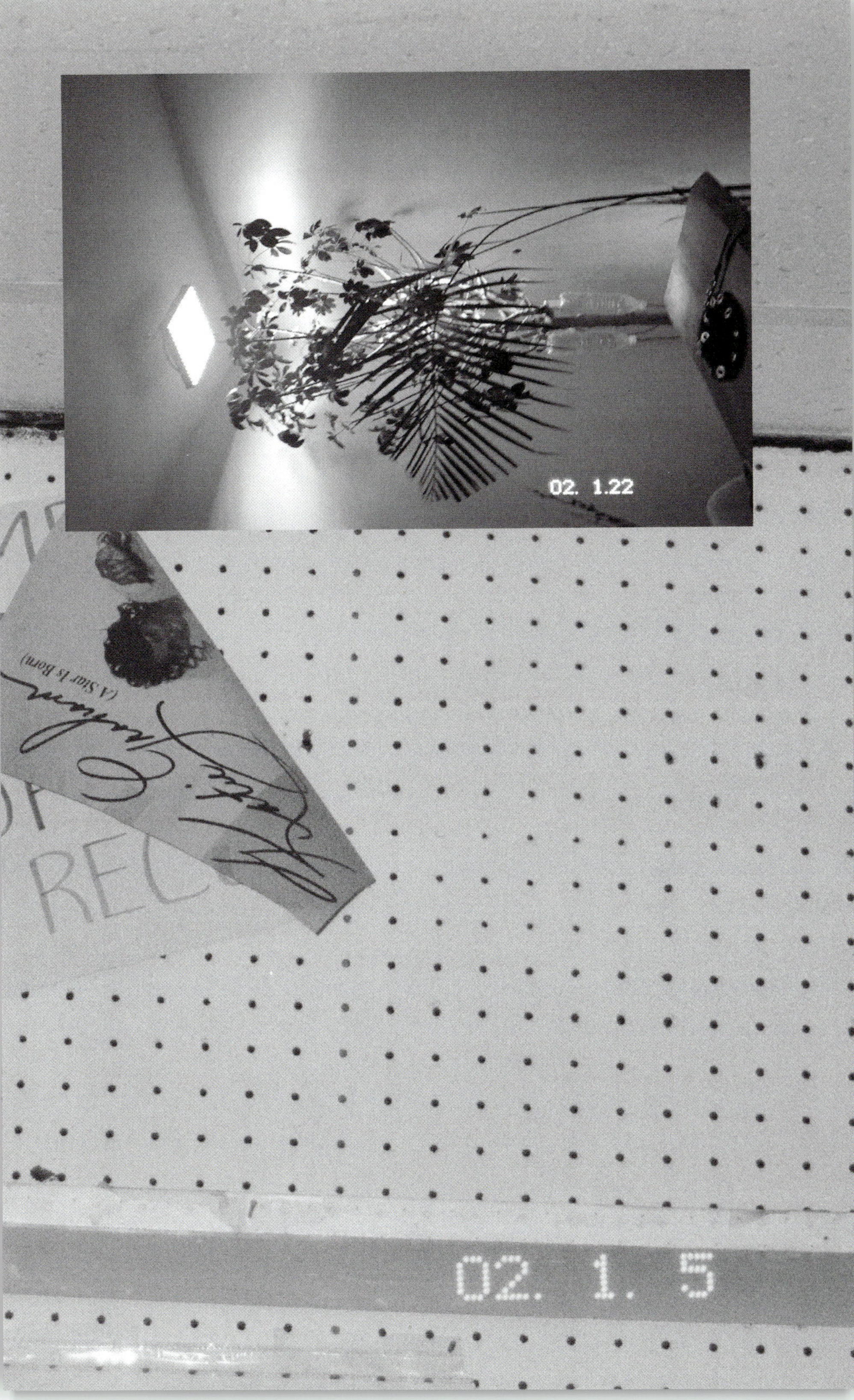
02. 1.22
(A Star Is Born)
02. 1. 5

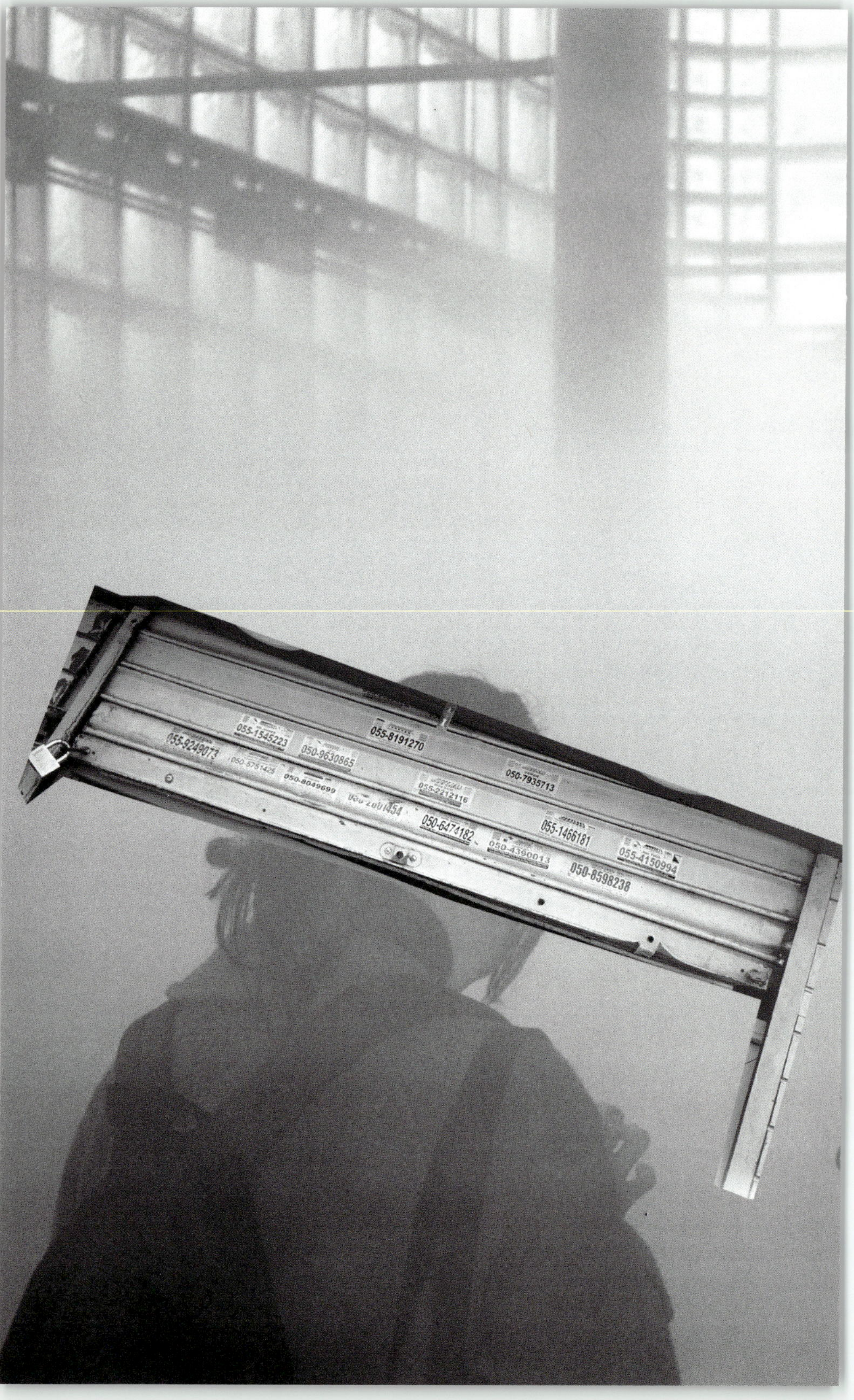
055-8191270
055-1545223
055-9249073
050-9630865
050-7935713
055-2212116
050-6474182
055-1466181
055-4150994
050-8598238

I HOPE HE KNOWS I'LL NEVER FORGIVE HIM. MEN ARE THE FUCKING WORST.

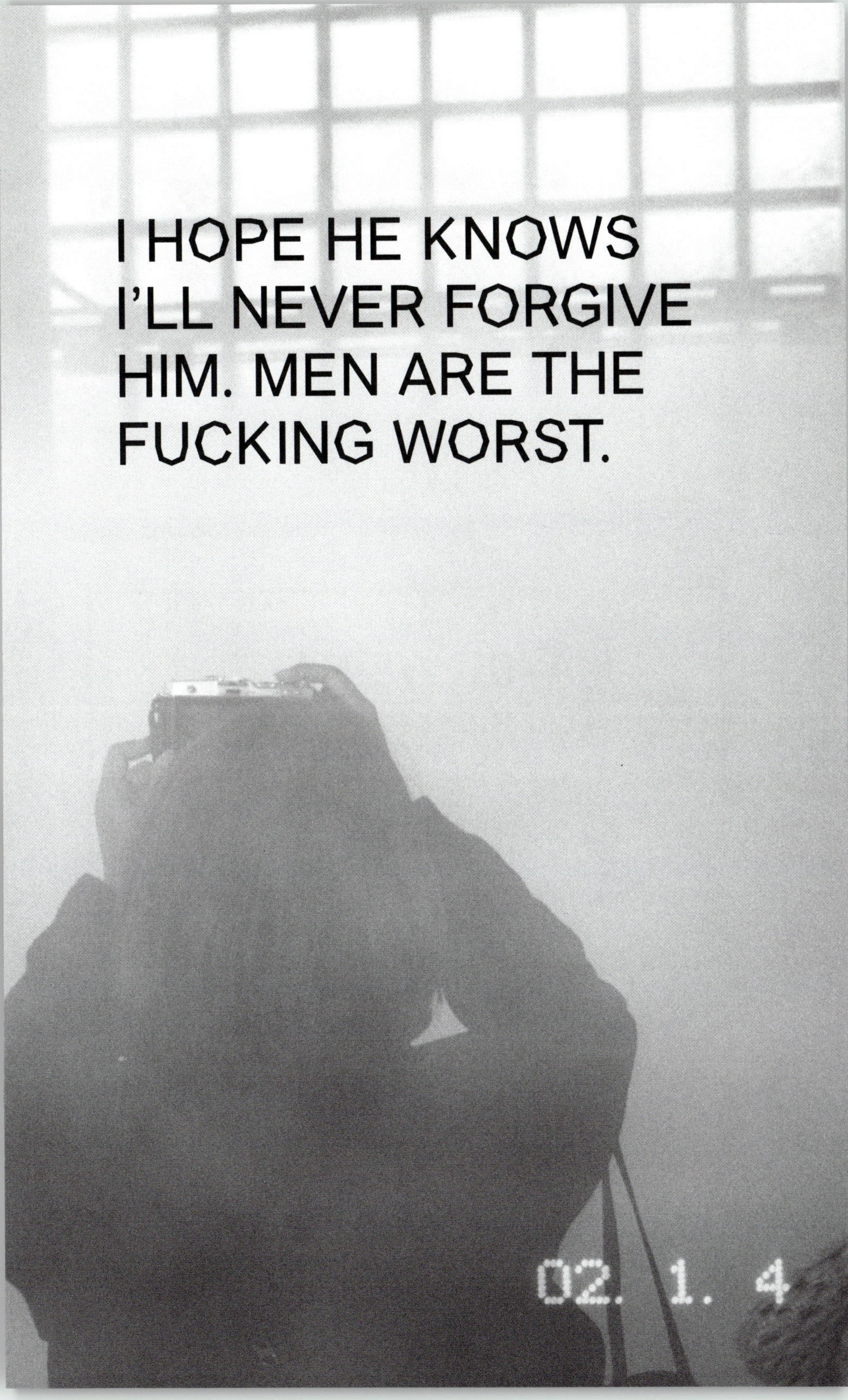

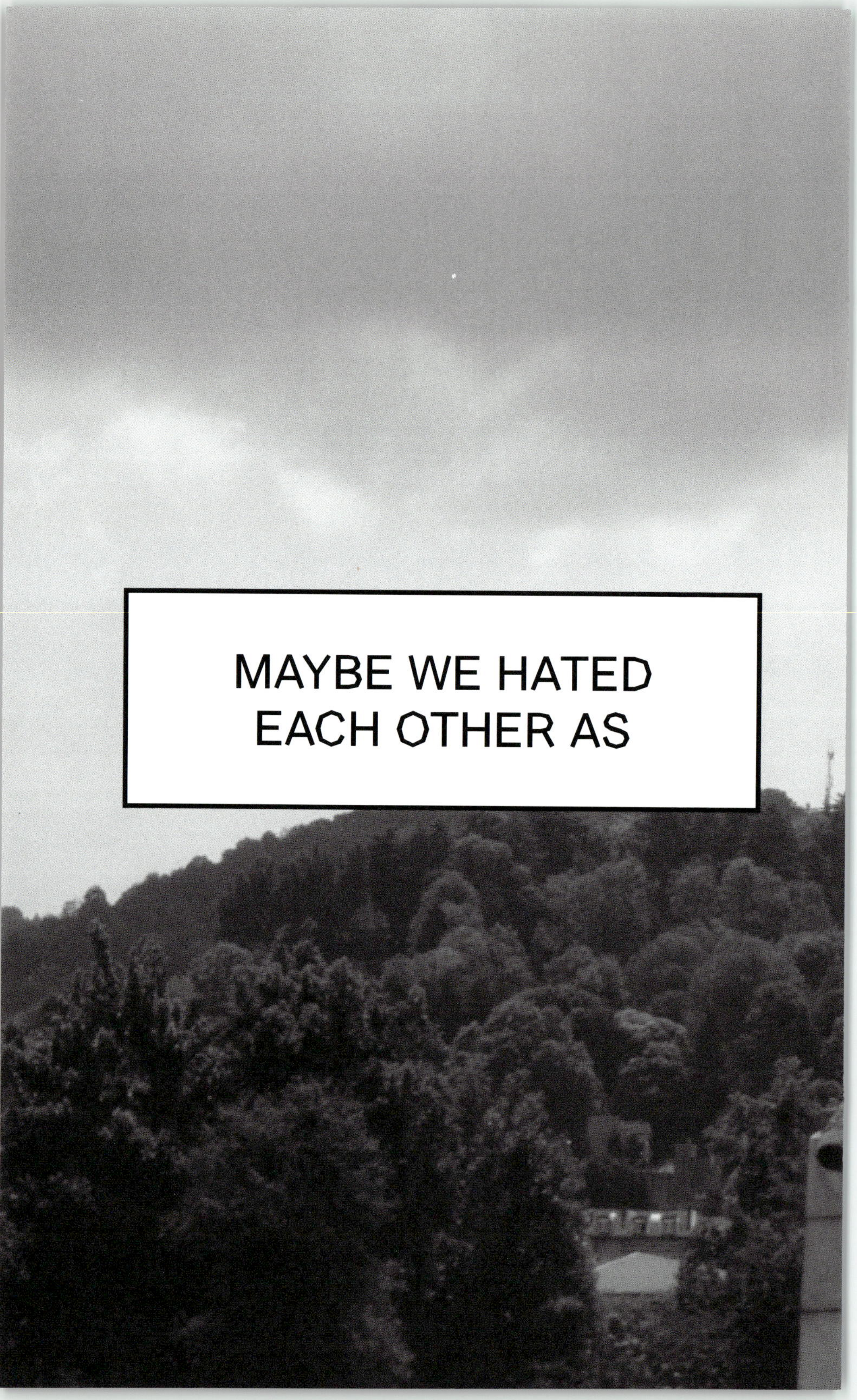
MAYBE WE HATED
EACH OTHER AS

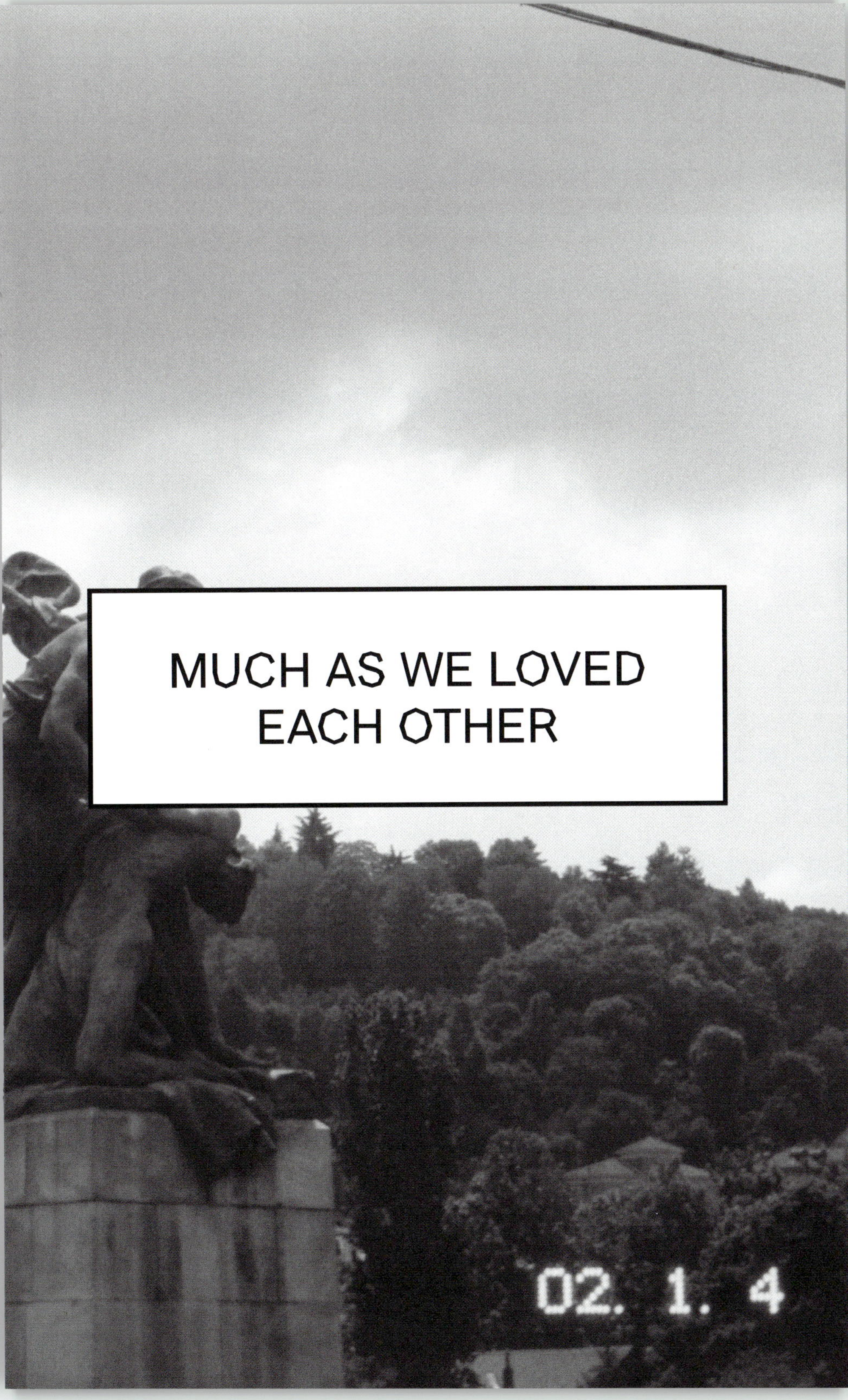
MUCH AS WE LOVED
EACH OTHER
02. 1. 4

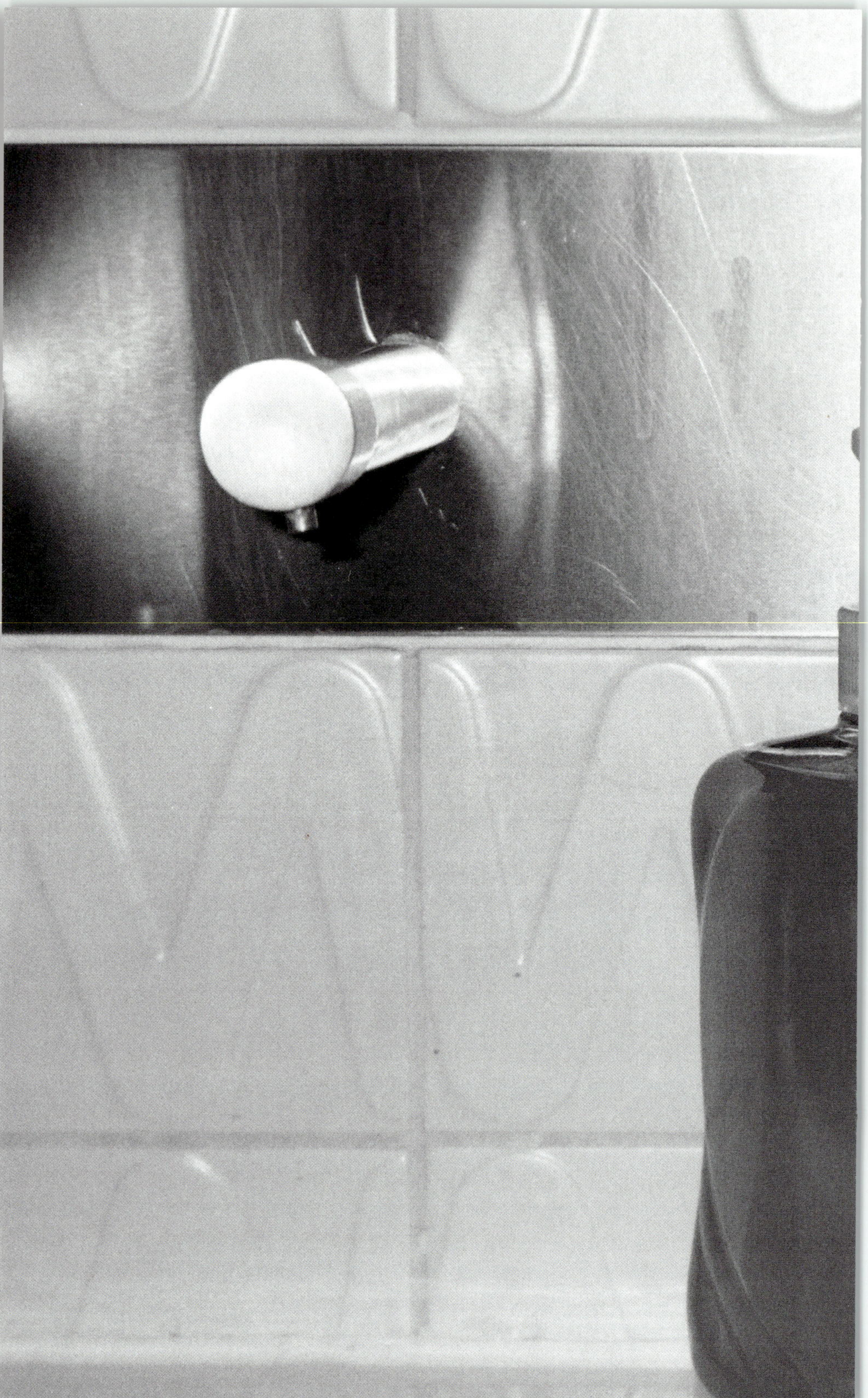

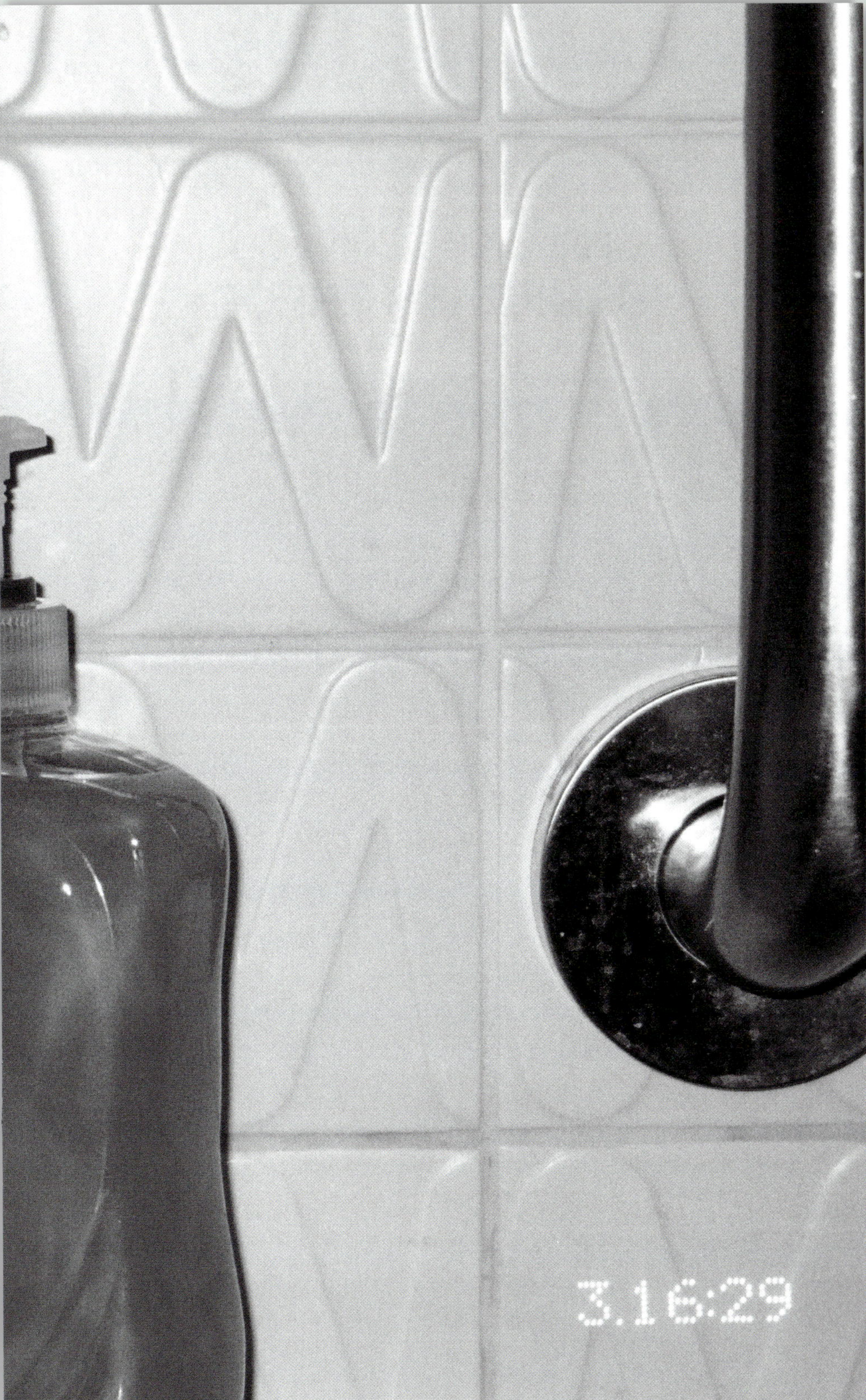
3.16:29

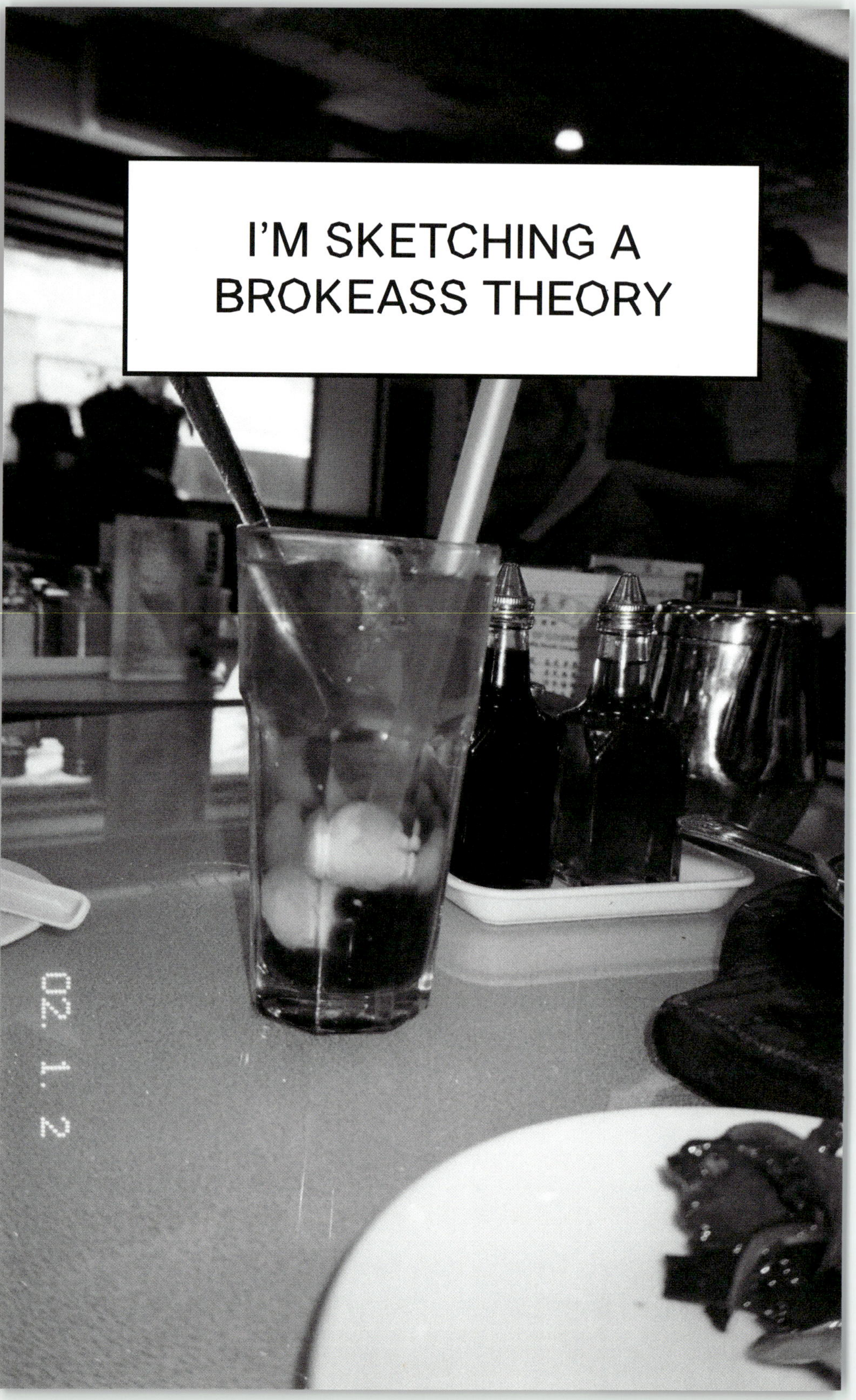
I'M SKETCHING A
BROKEASS THEORY
02. 1. 2

OF COLORED GIRLS WHO WILL NEVER FIT

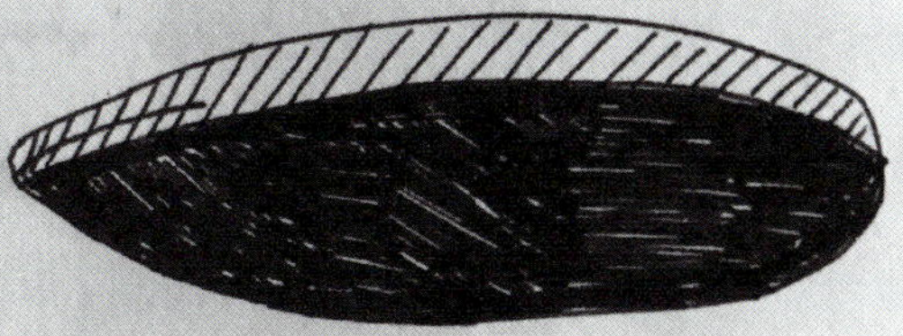

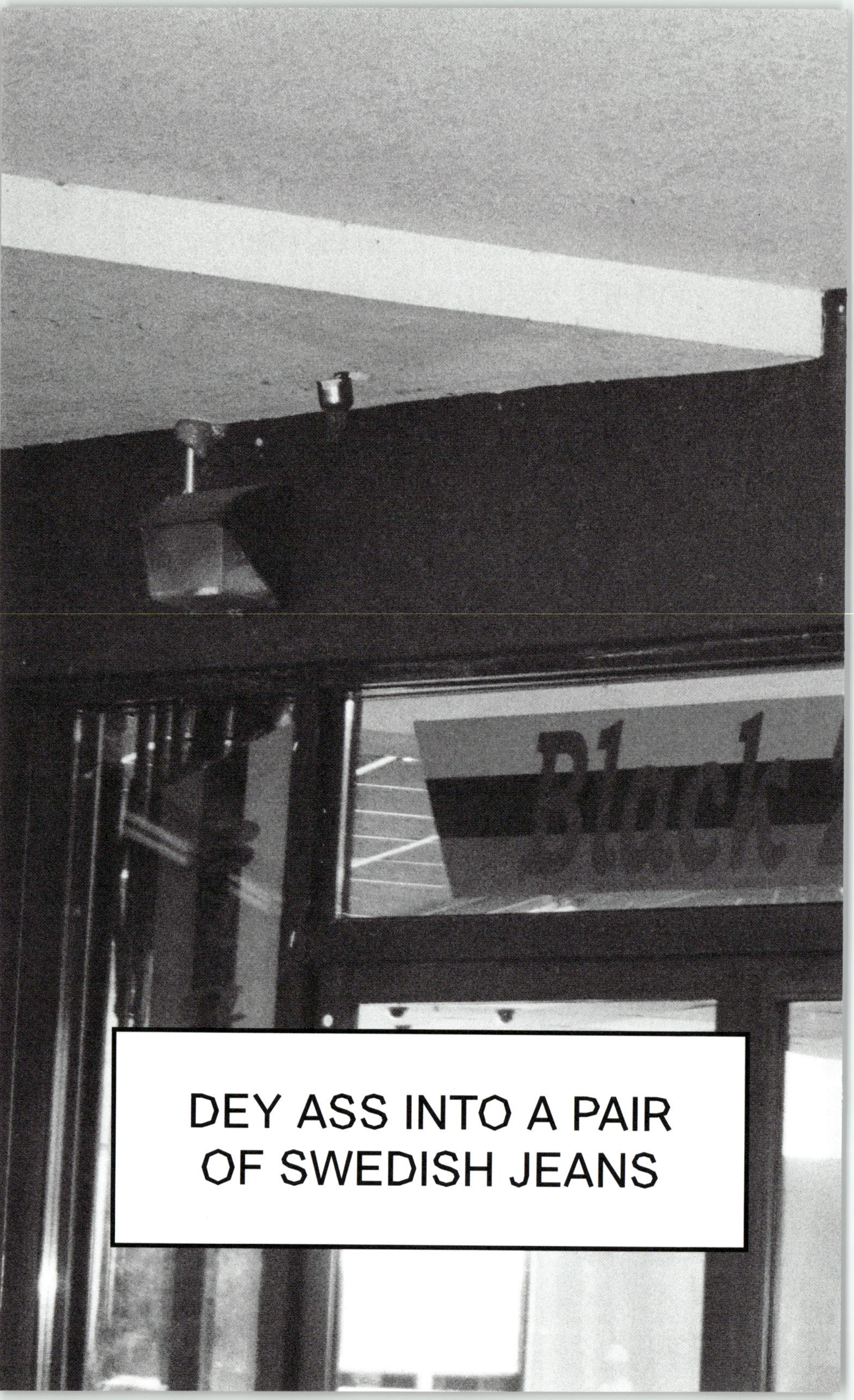
DEY ASS INTO A PAIR
OF SWEDISH JEANS

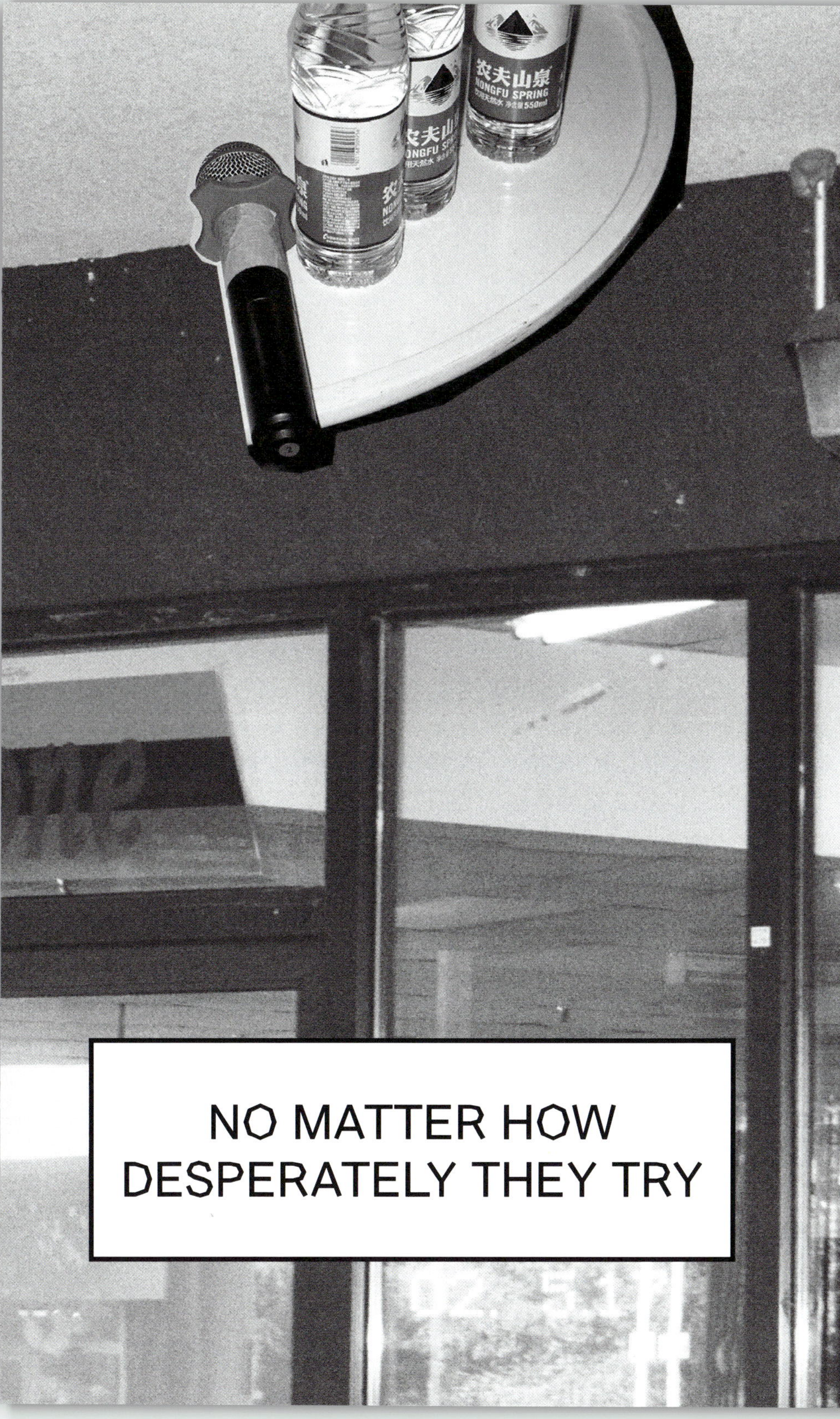

NO MATTER HOW
DESPERATELY THEY TRY

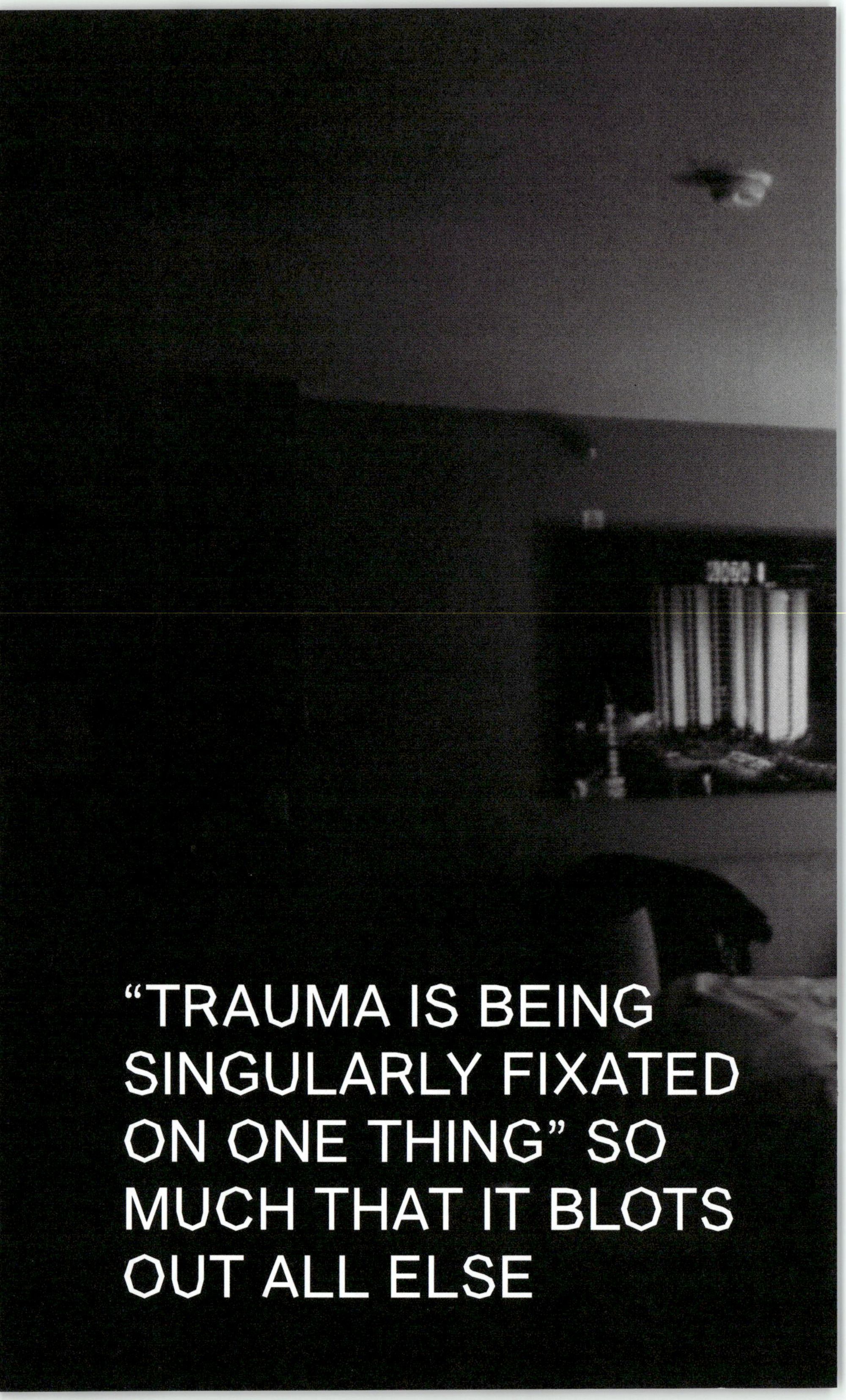

"TRAUMA IS BEING SINGULARLY FIXATED ON ONE THING" SO MUCH THAT IT BLOTS OUT ALL ELSE

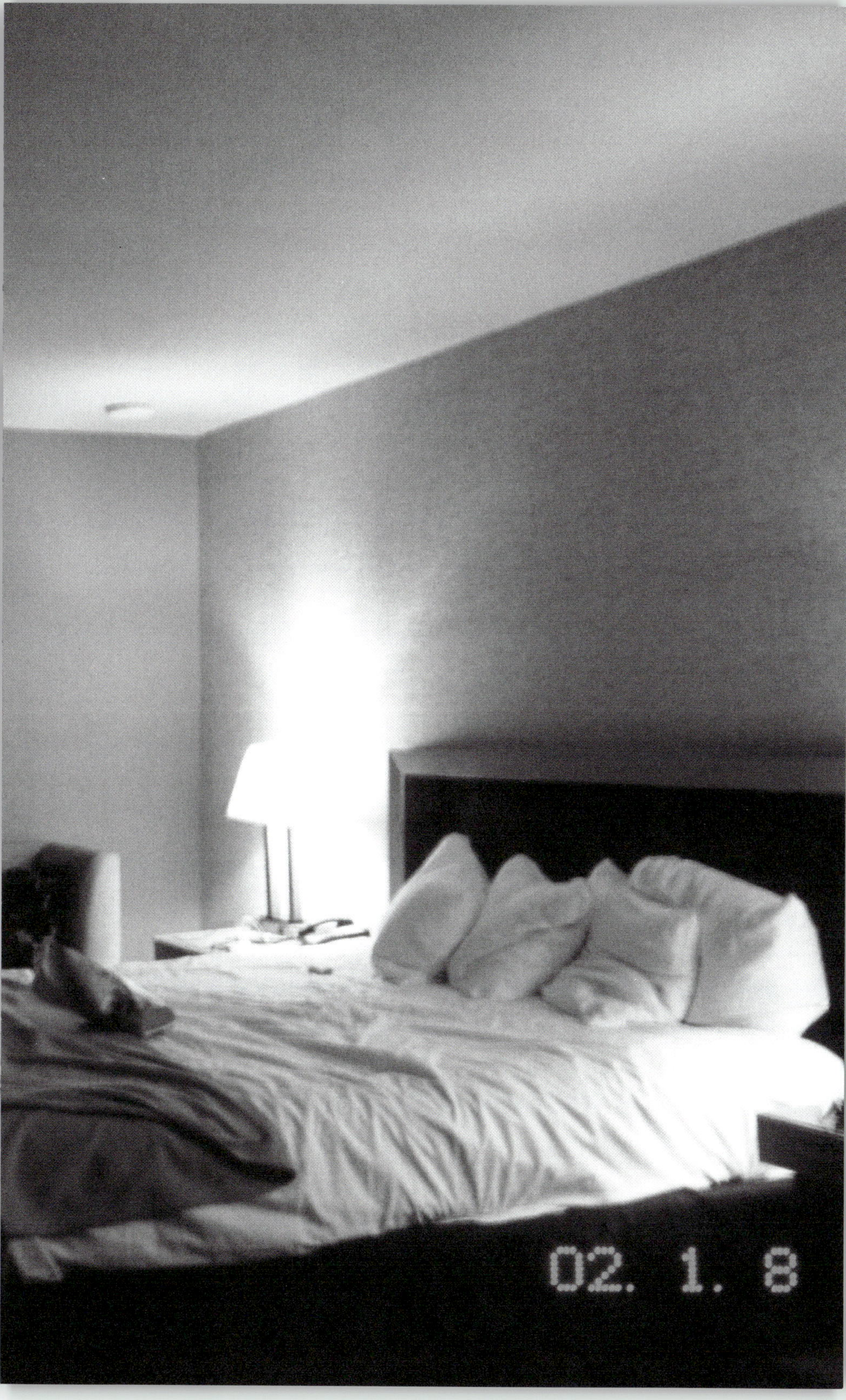
02. 1. 8

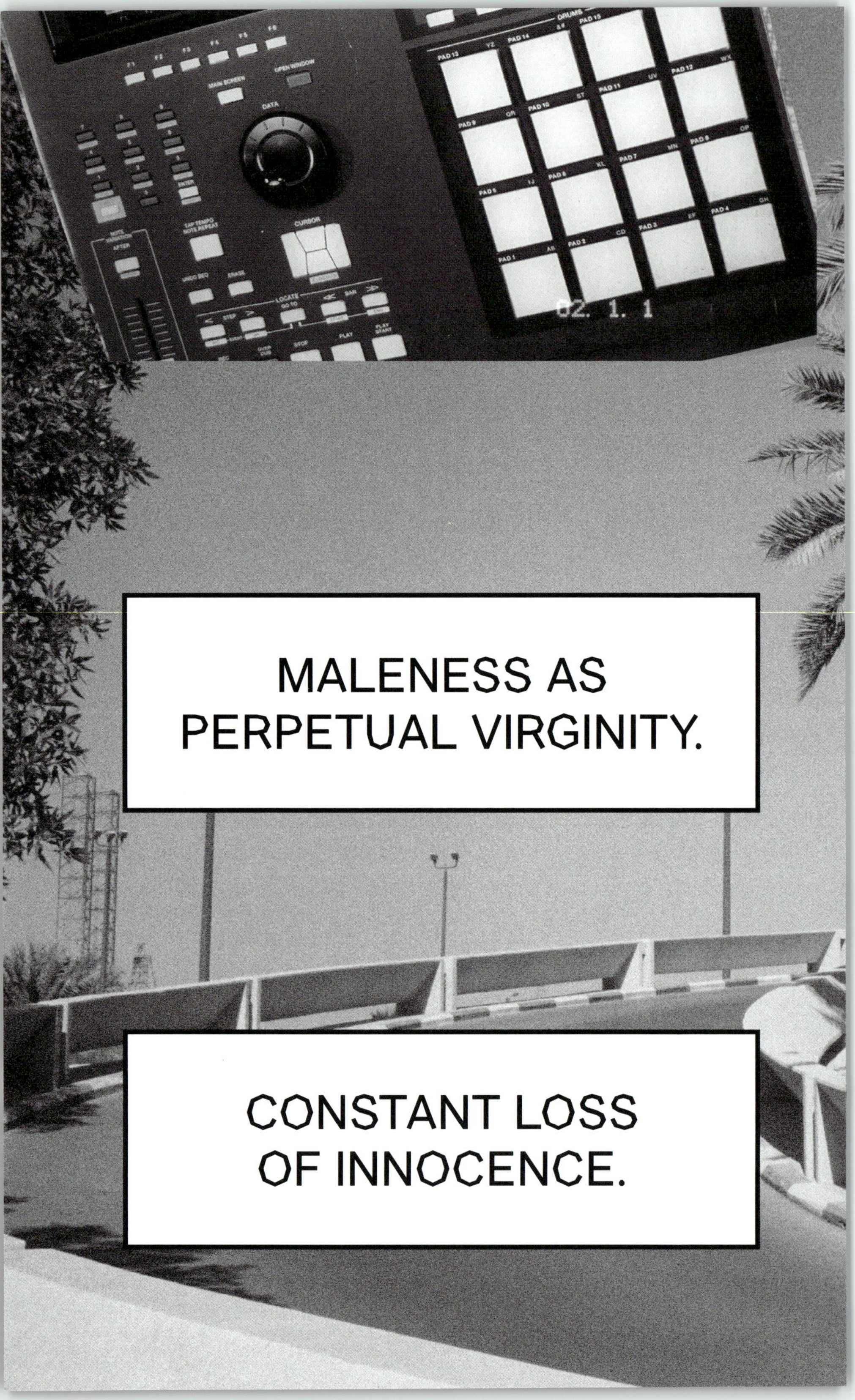
MALENESS AS PERPETUAL VIRGINITY.
CONSTANT LOSS OF INNOCENCE.

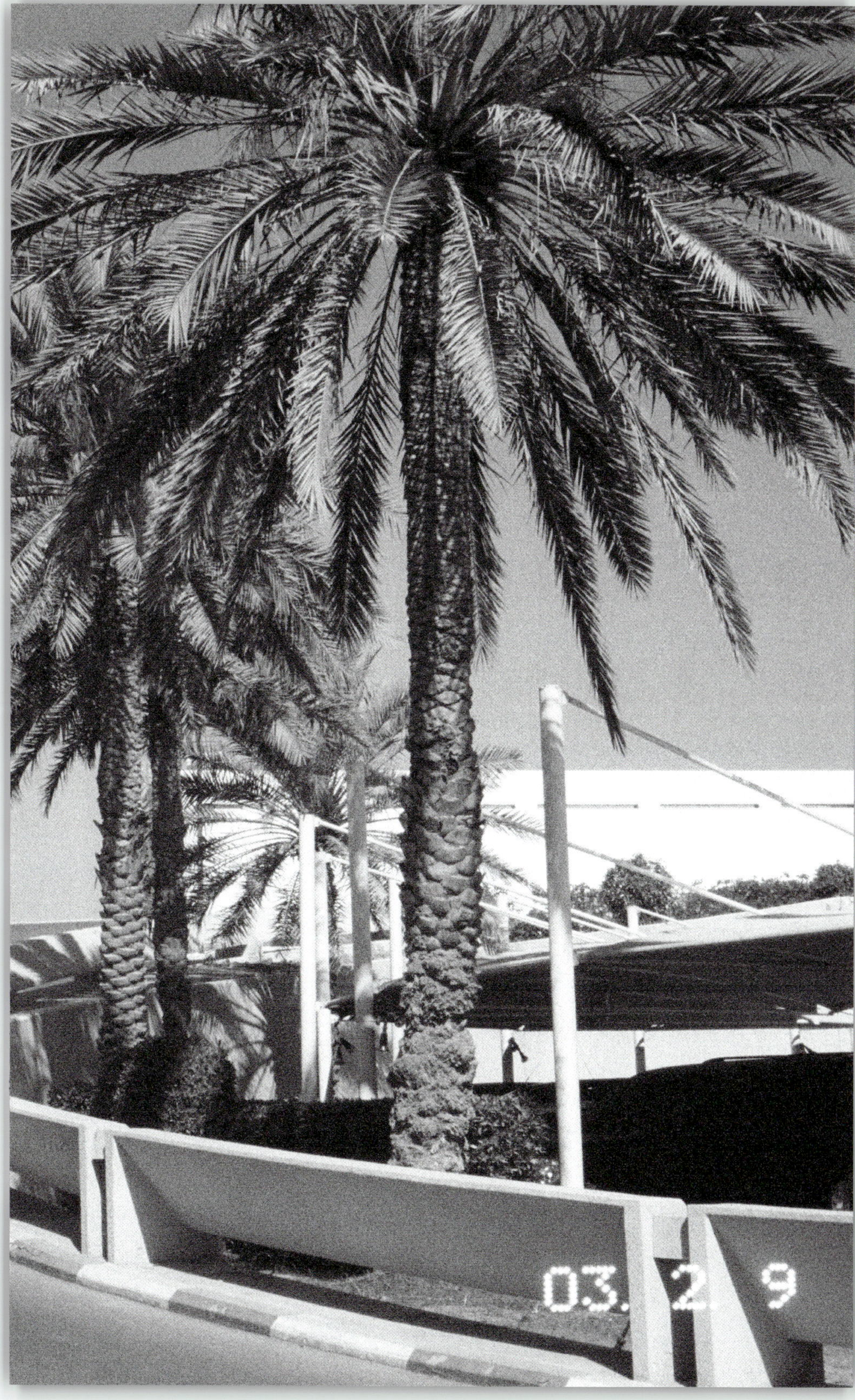
03. 2. 9

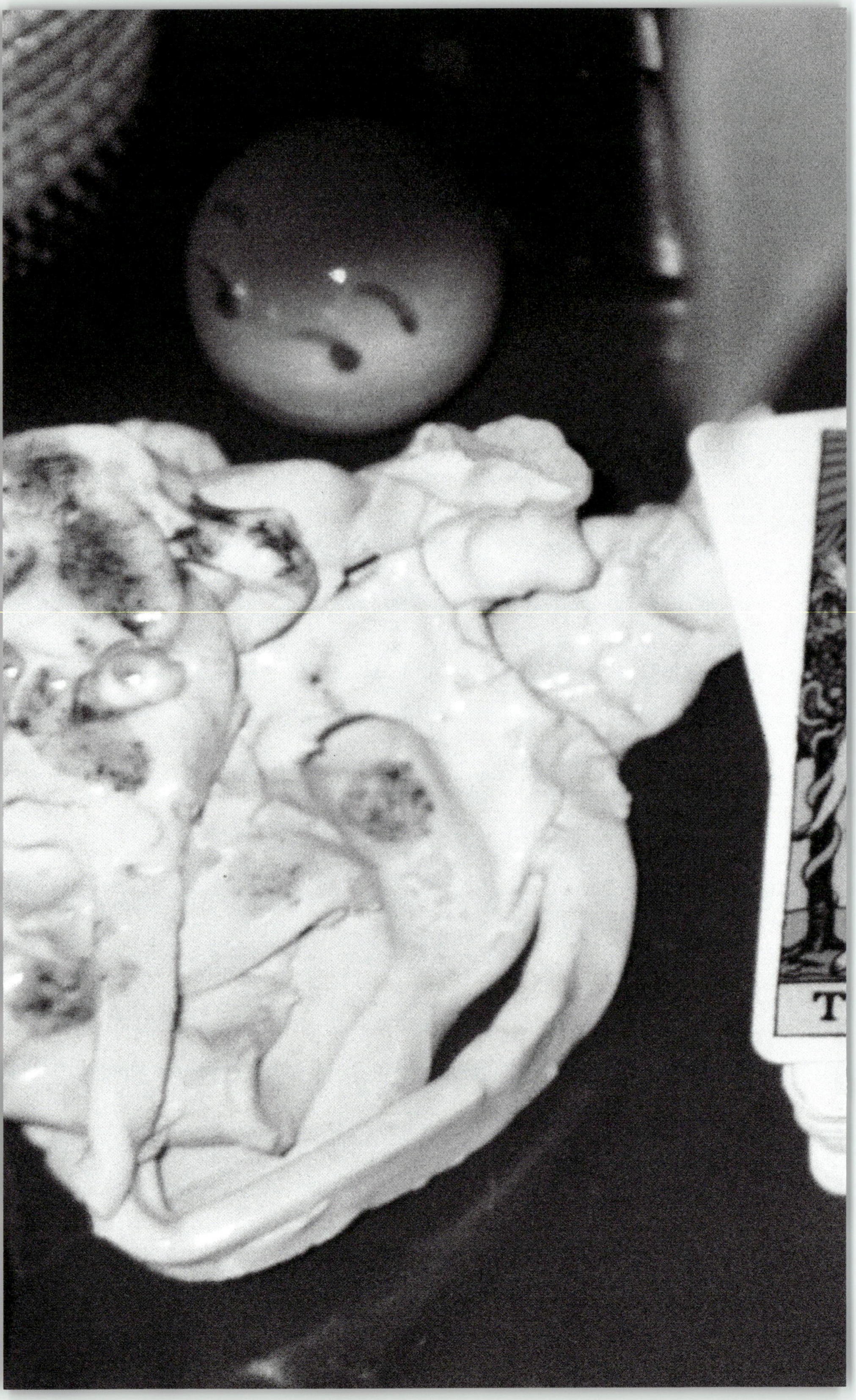

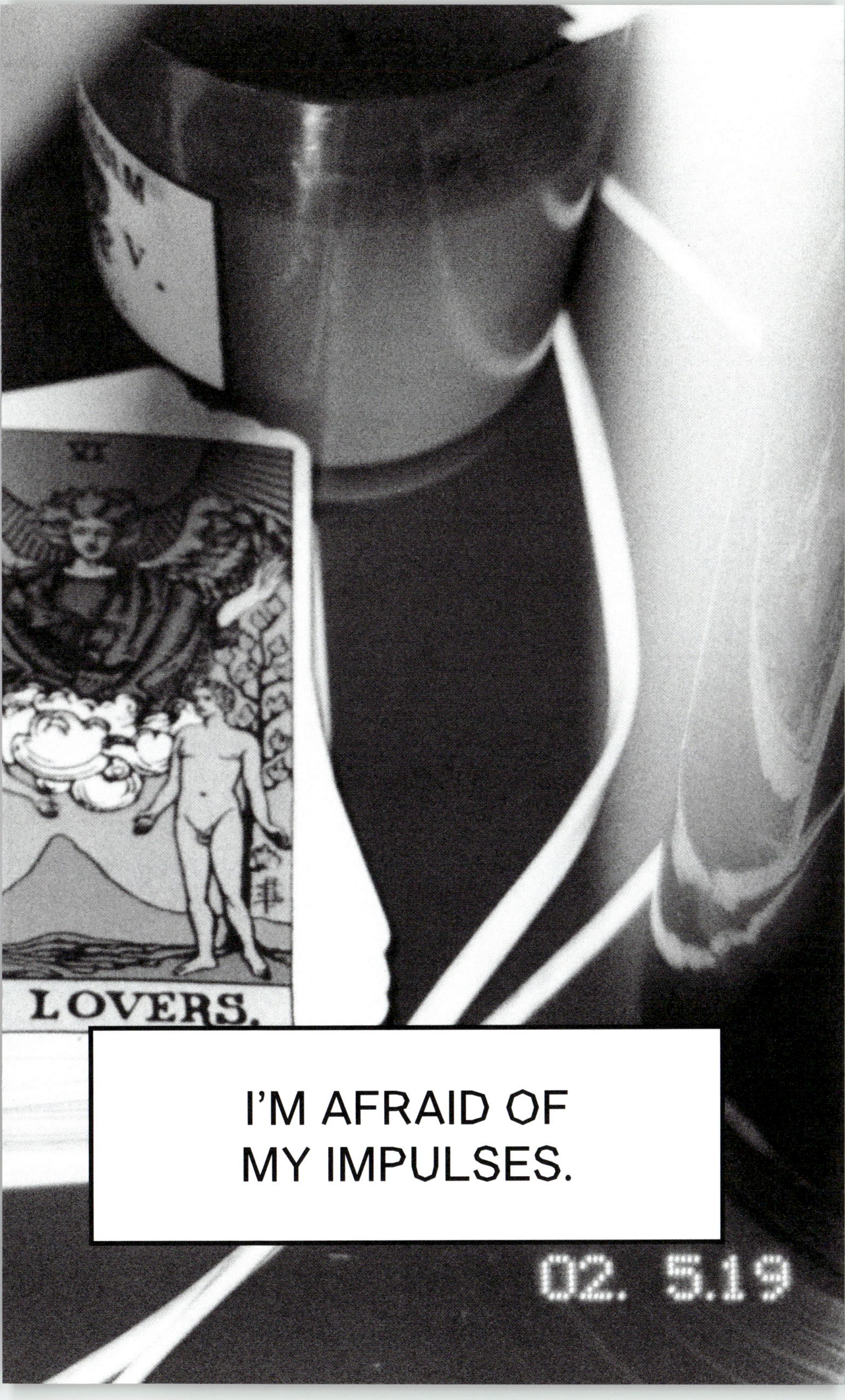
LOVERS.
I'M AFRAID OF
MY IMPULSES.
02. 5.19

AM I GETTIN

YES

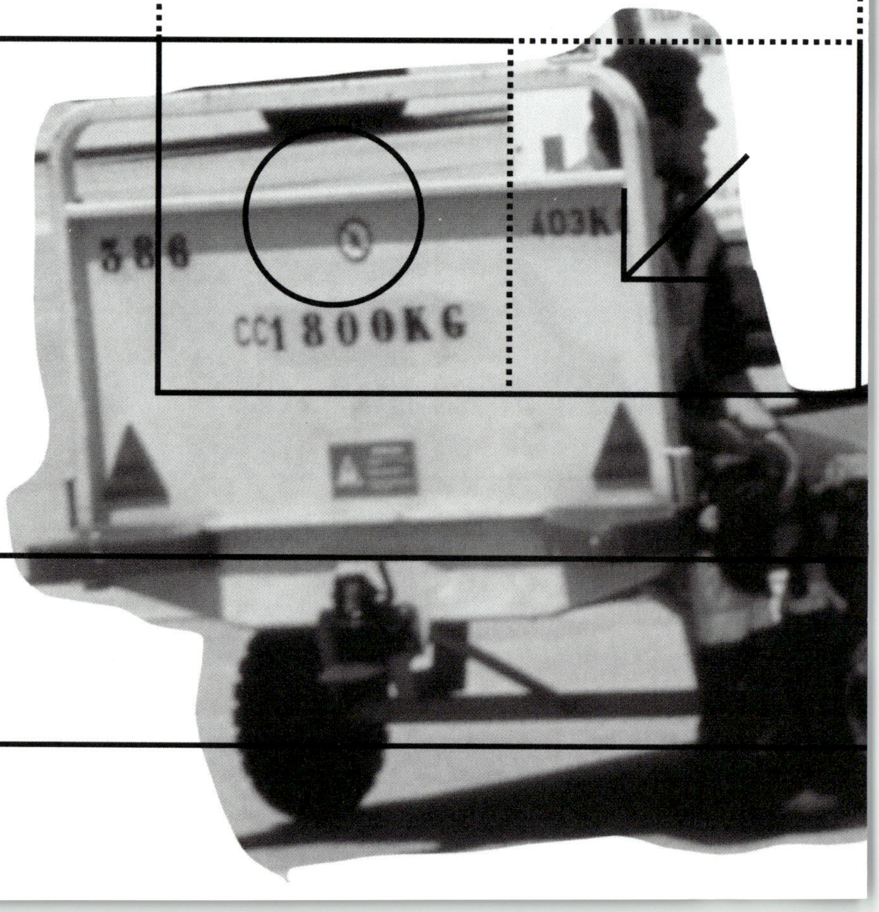

G FAT ?

FEAR OF

NO

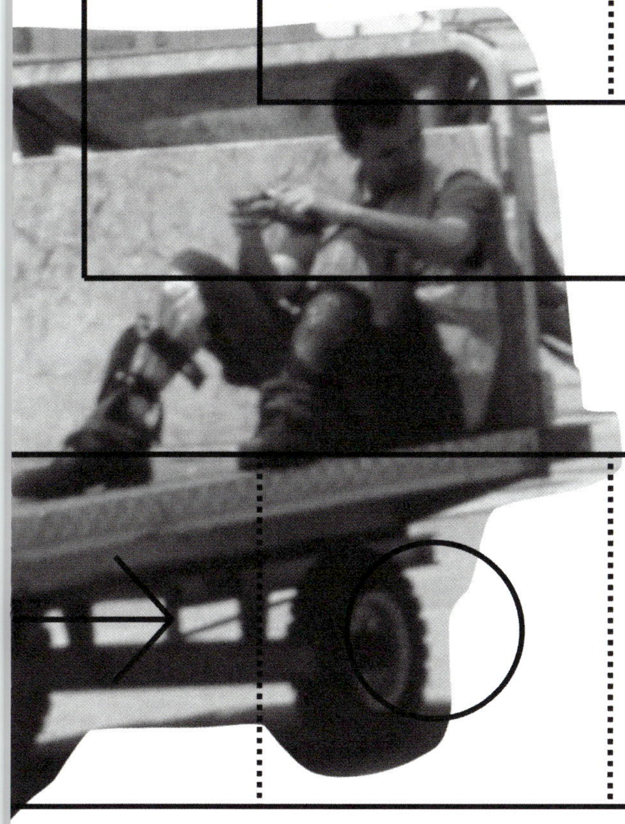

BEING BROKE

I CAN'T TELL
ANYMORE !!

WHY DON'T THE

$$$$$$

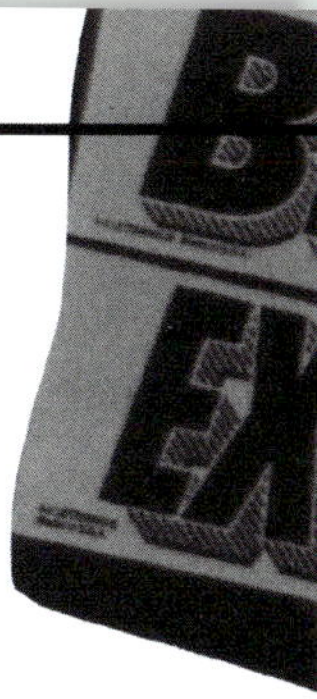

I'M

MY CLOTHES
ARE BAGGIER

LOVE ME ?

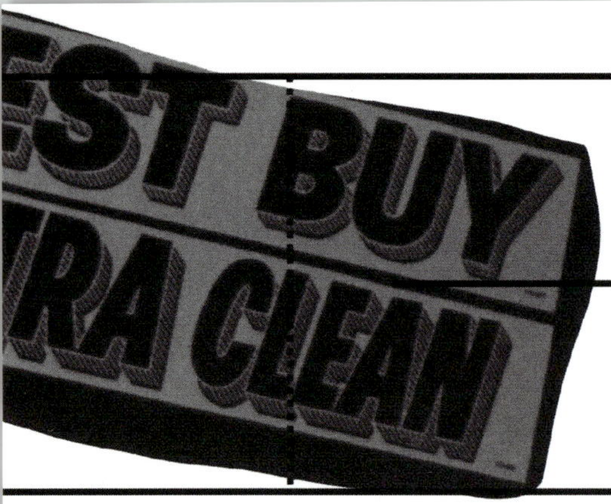

AND YET I
WEIGH MORE

THEY ARE
STOOOPID

PRIORIT

I HAVE BODY DYSMORPHIA

ES

NNNNNNNE

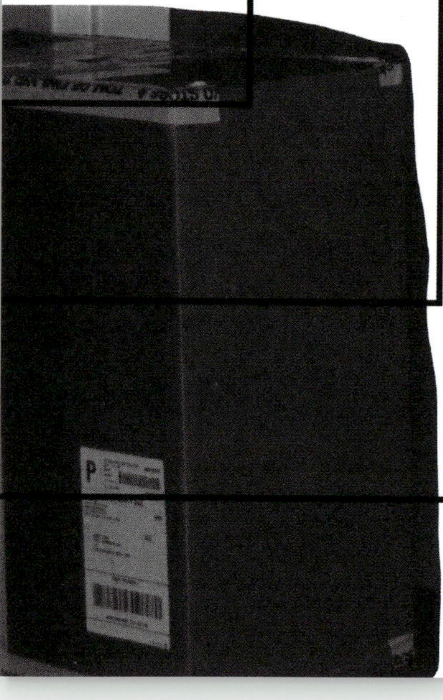

I HAVE SO MUCH I

IT
O

I

UCKING WORK 2 DO

'S A
OMPULSION

↘

—

GO SLOW

AM THE BALL

←

NO NO NO

LET'S DO
OTHING !!!

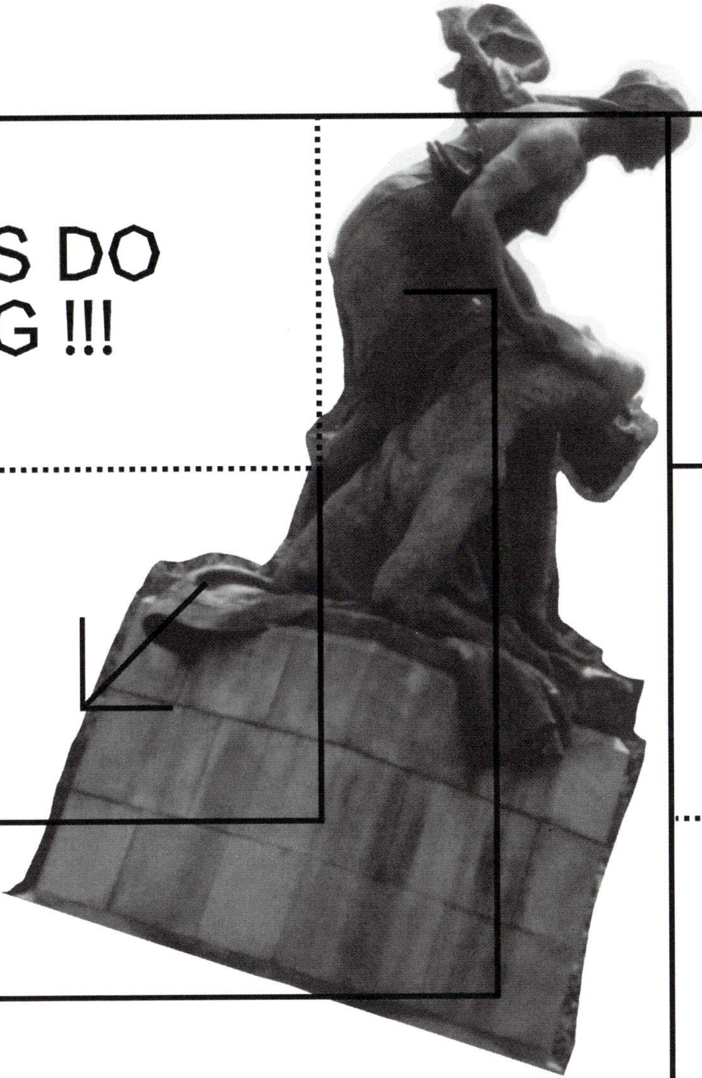

YI

D BAD GIRL

S I DO BITCH

←

U AIN'T GOT T

IENDLY P !

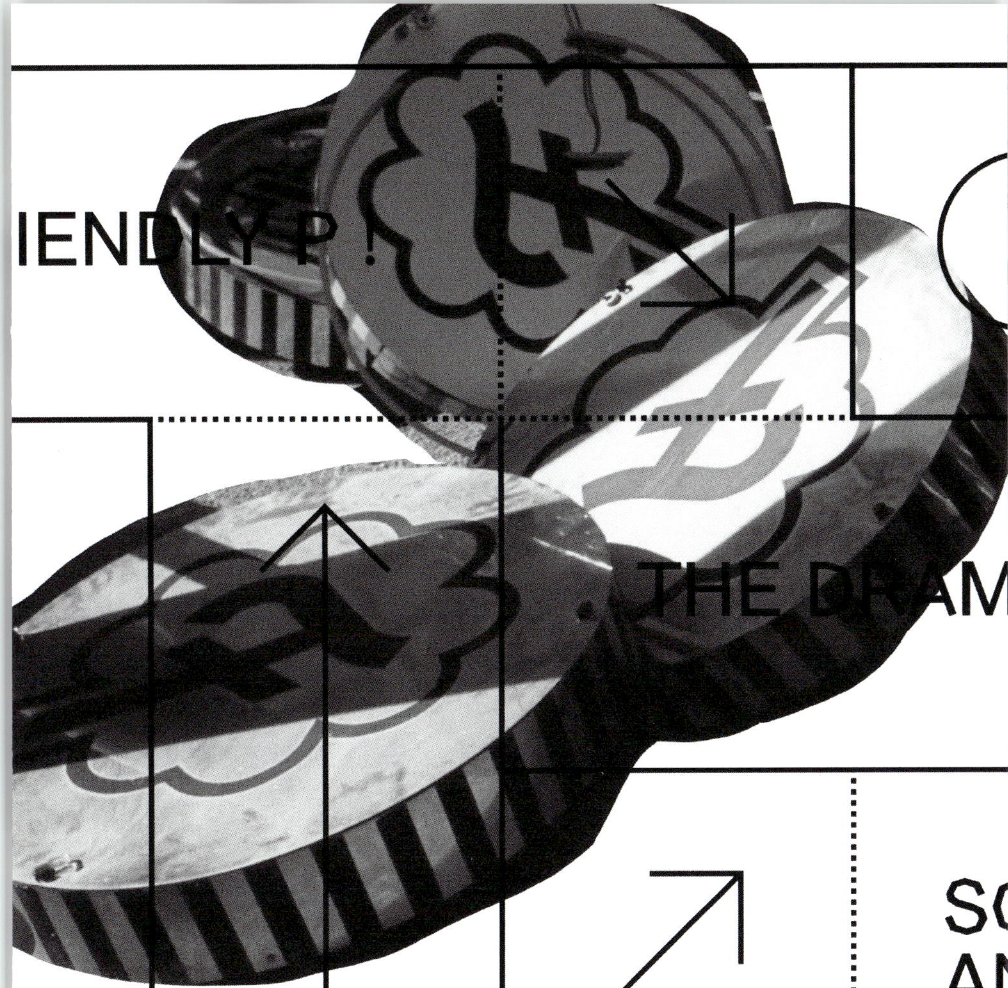

THE DRAM

SO
AN

ME 4 BOOTY B

A

ME
ON P ?

ITCH

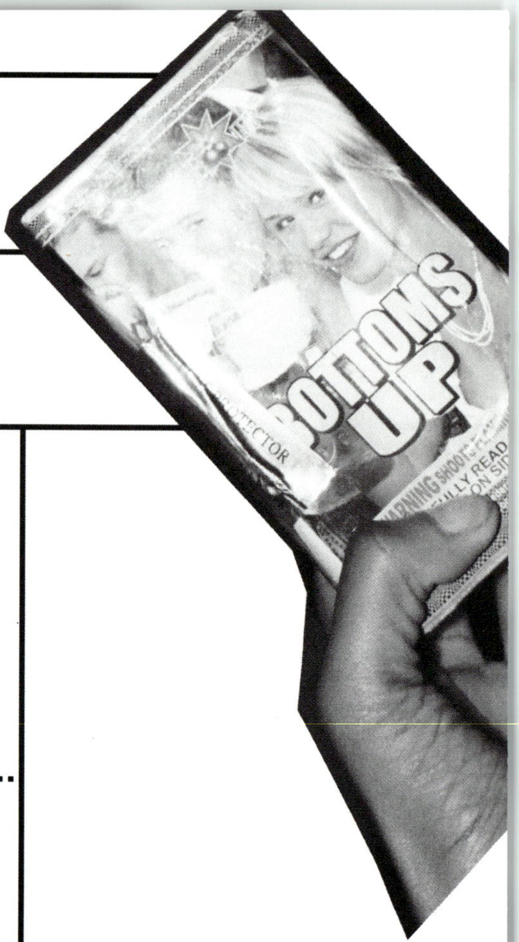

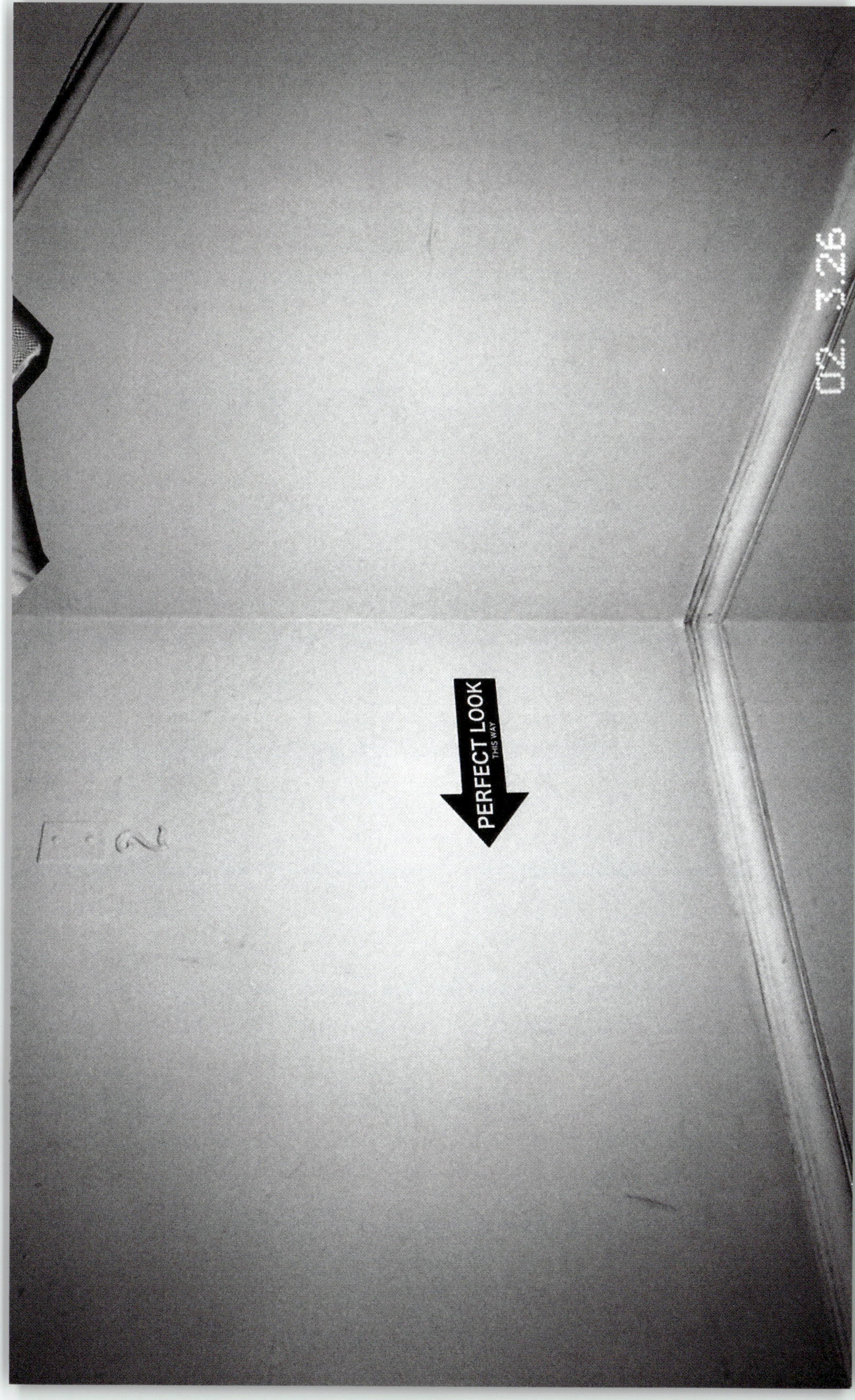
PERFECT LOOK
THIS WAY
02 3.26

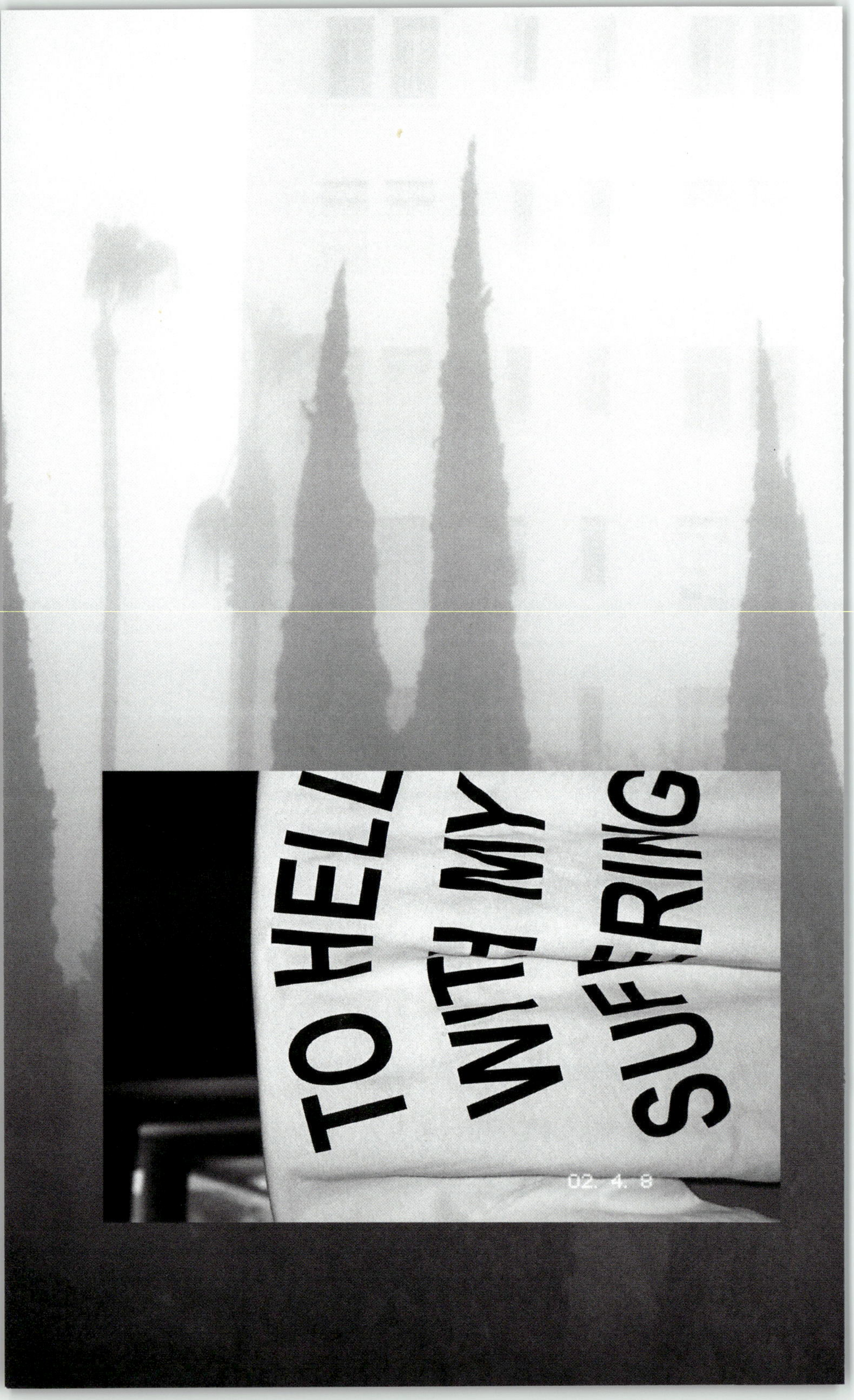
TO HELL
WITH MY
SUFFERING
02. 4. 8

optimism

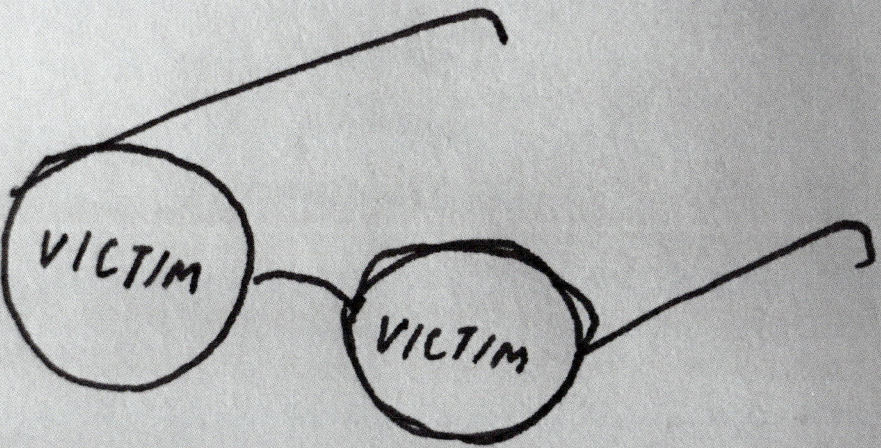

12 weeks

3 GOALS

TACTICS

DEADLINES

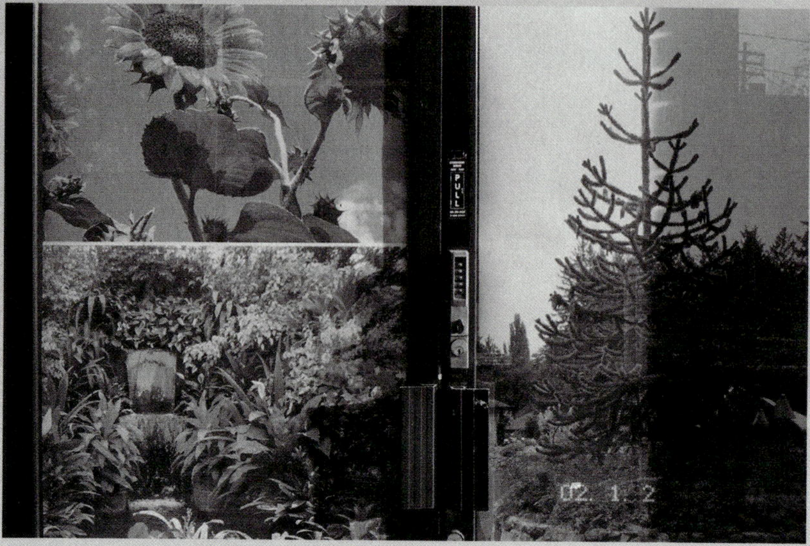
PULL

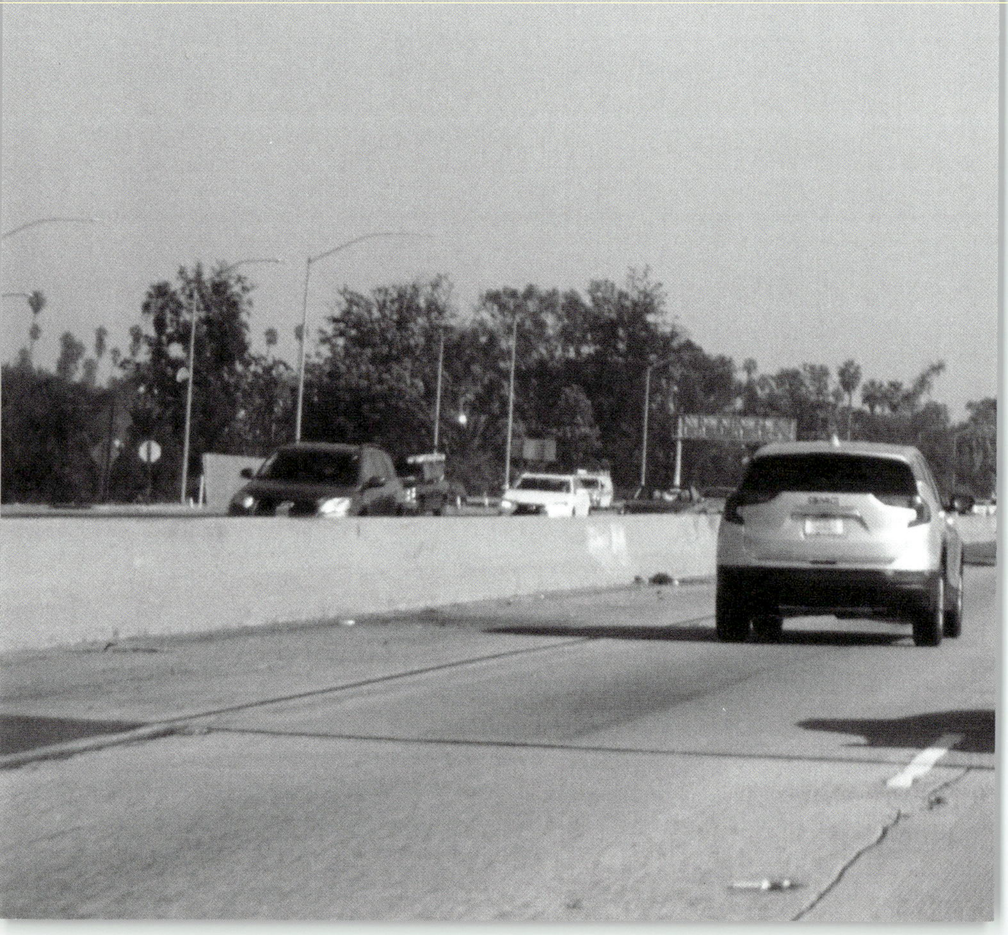

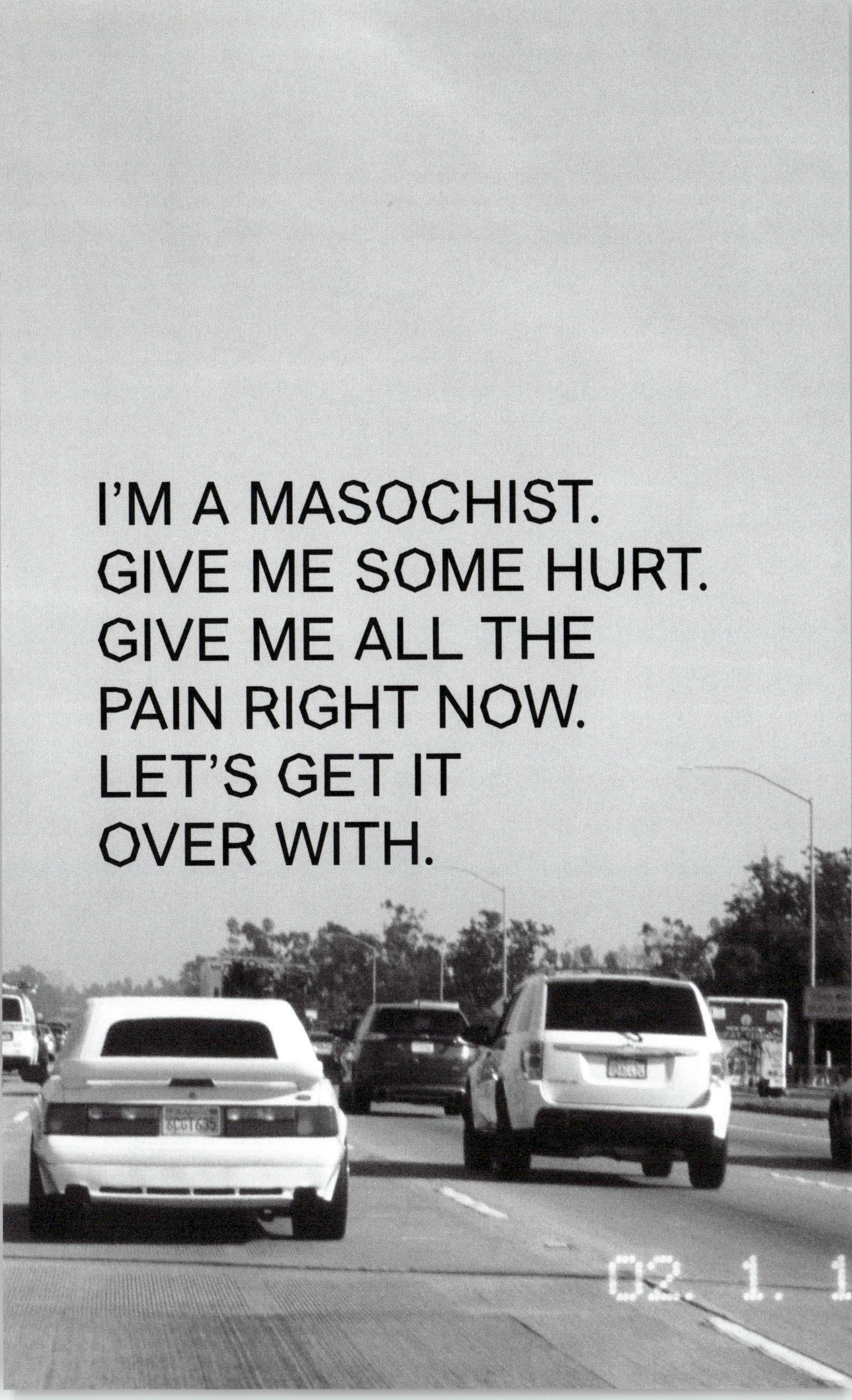
I'M A MASOCHIST.
GIVE ME SOME HURT.
GIVE ME ALL THE
PAIN RIGHT NOW.
LET'S GET IT
OVER WITH.
02. 1. 1

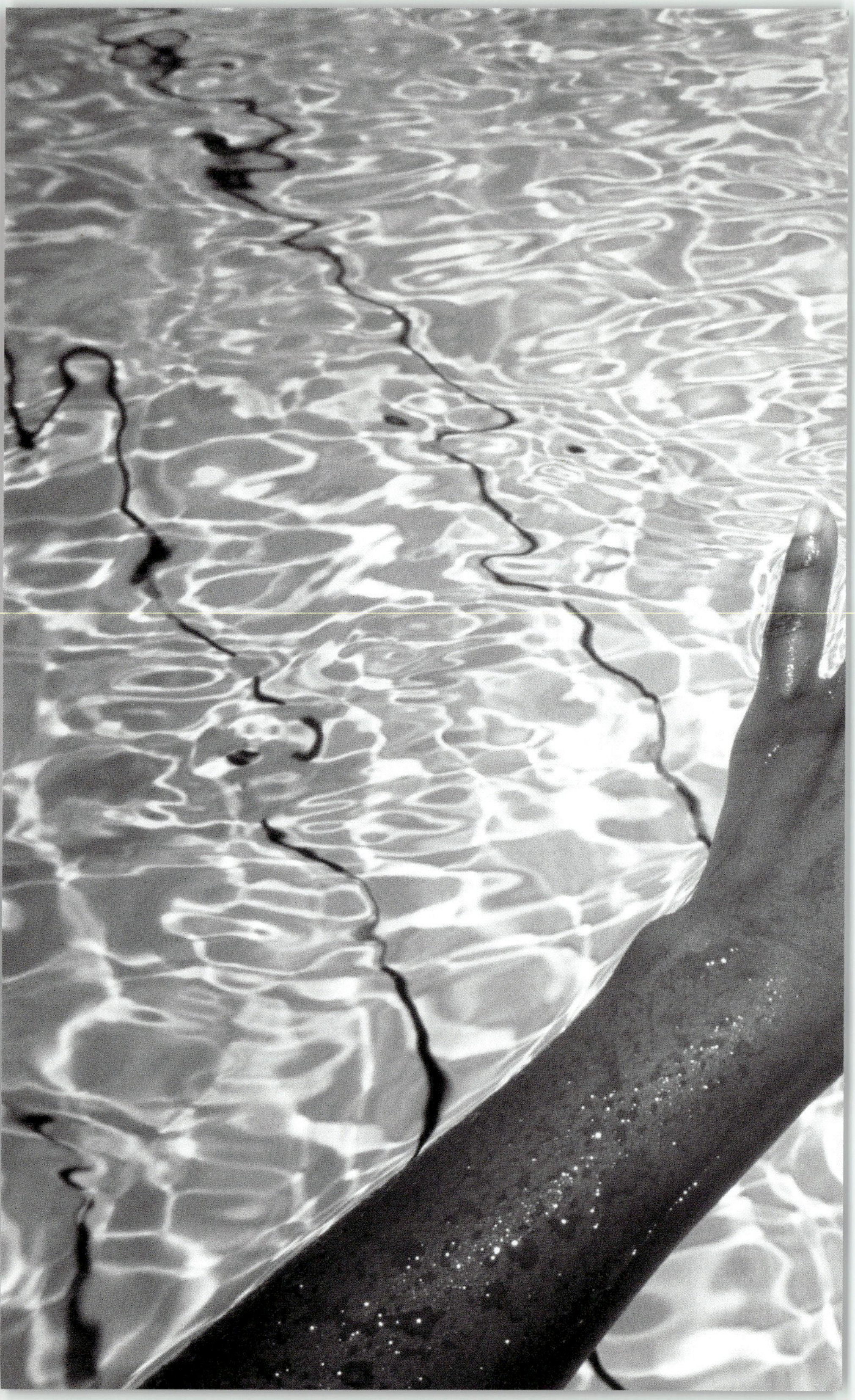

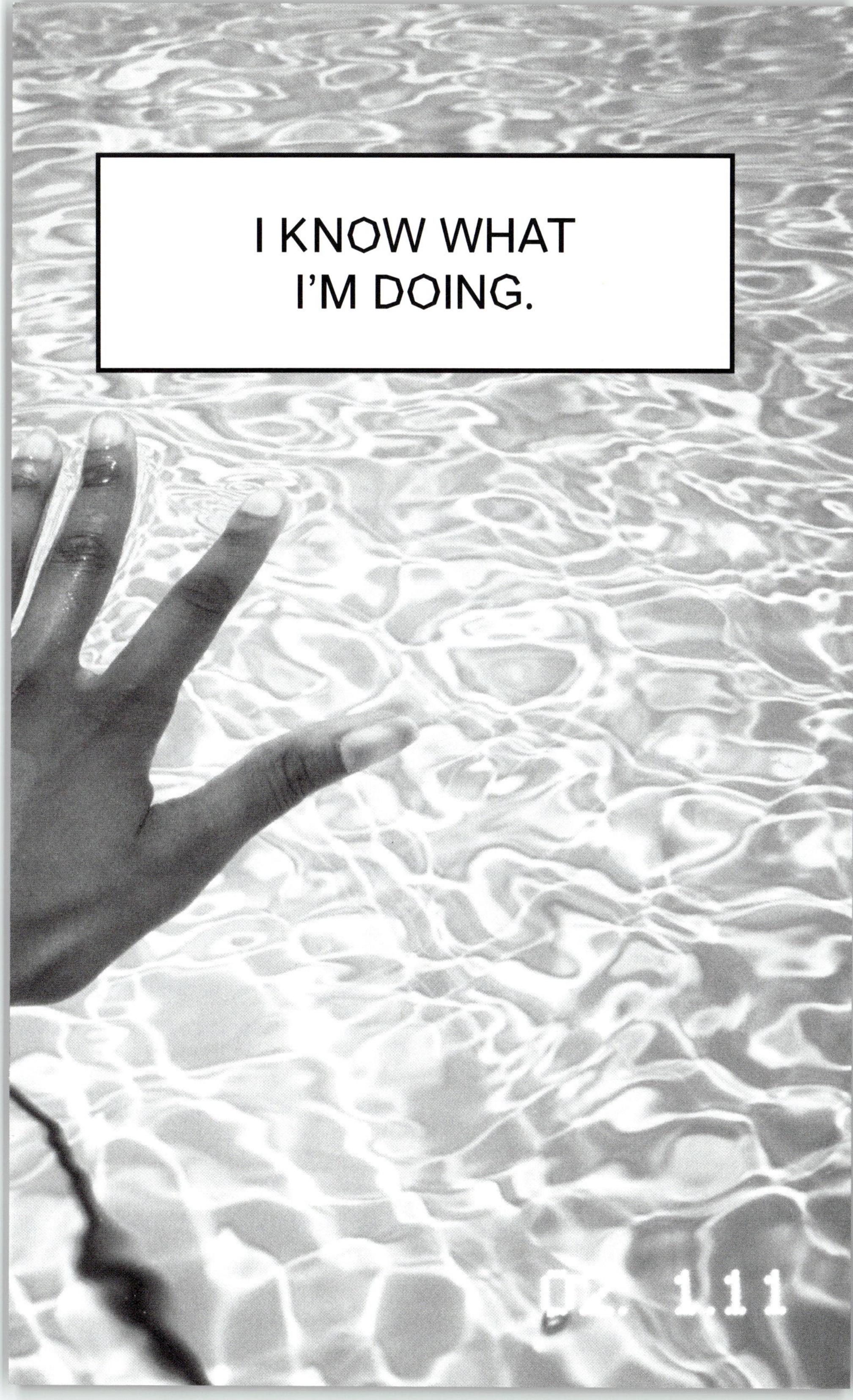
I KNOW WHAT
I'M DOING.

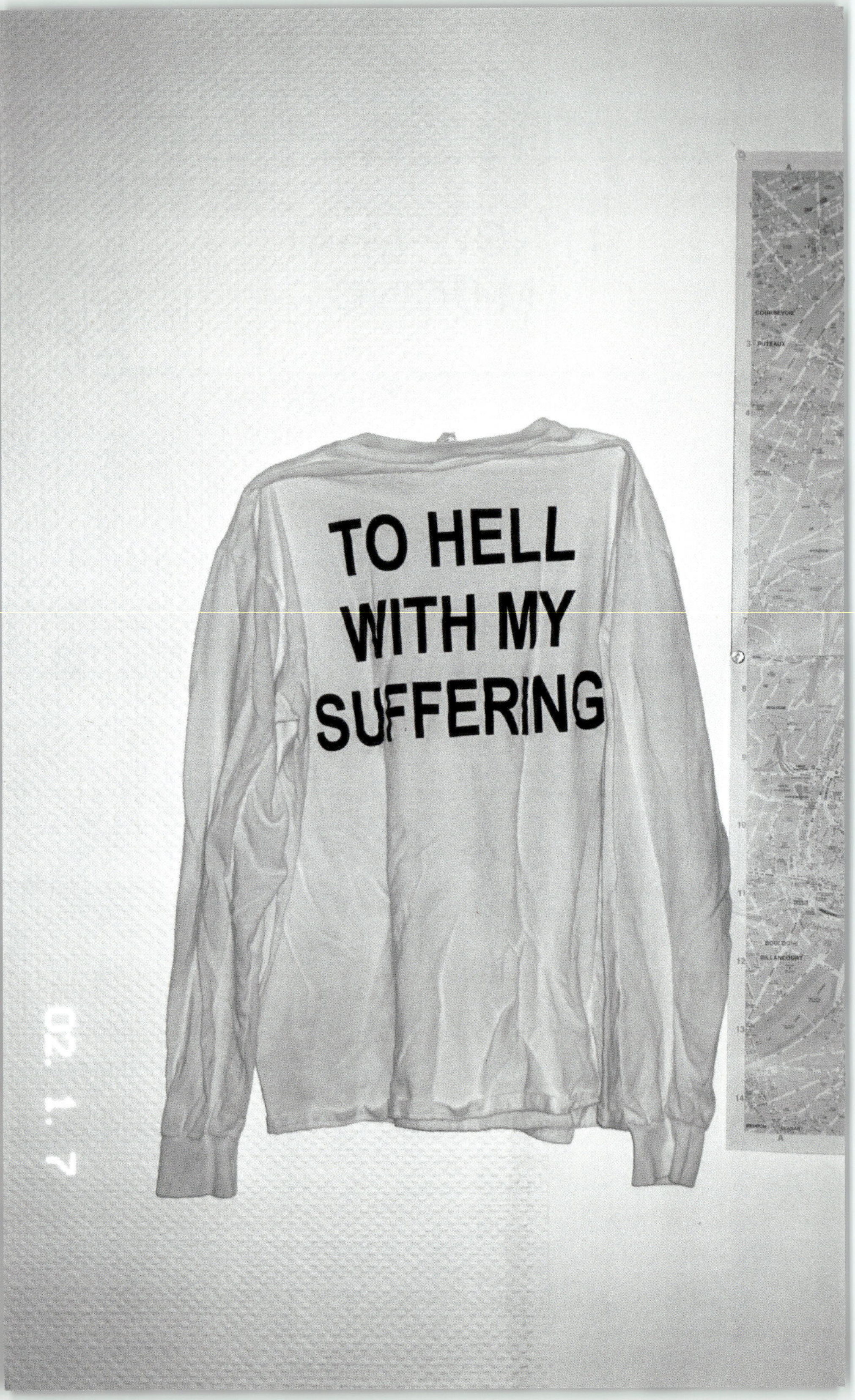
TO HELL
WITH MY
SUFFERING
02. 1. 7

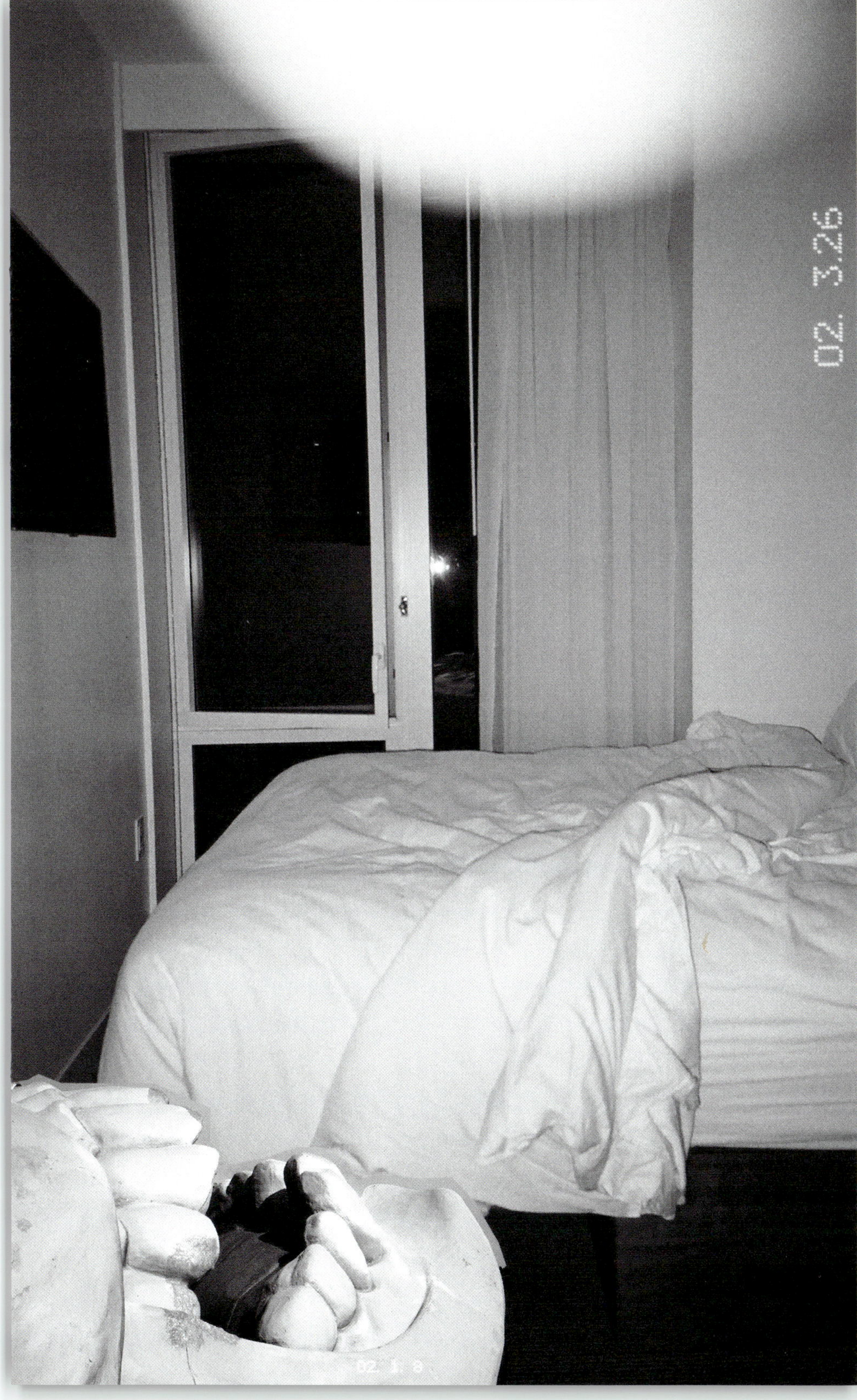
02. 3.26
02. 1. 8

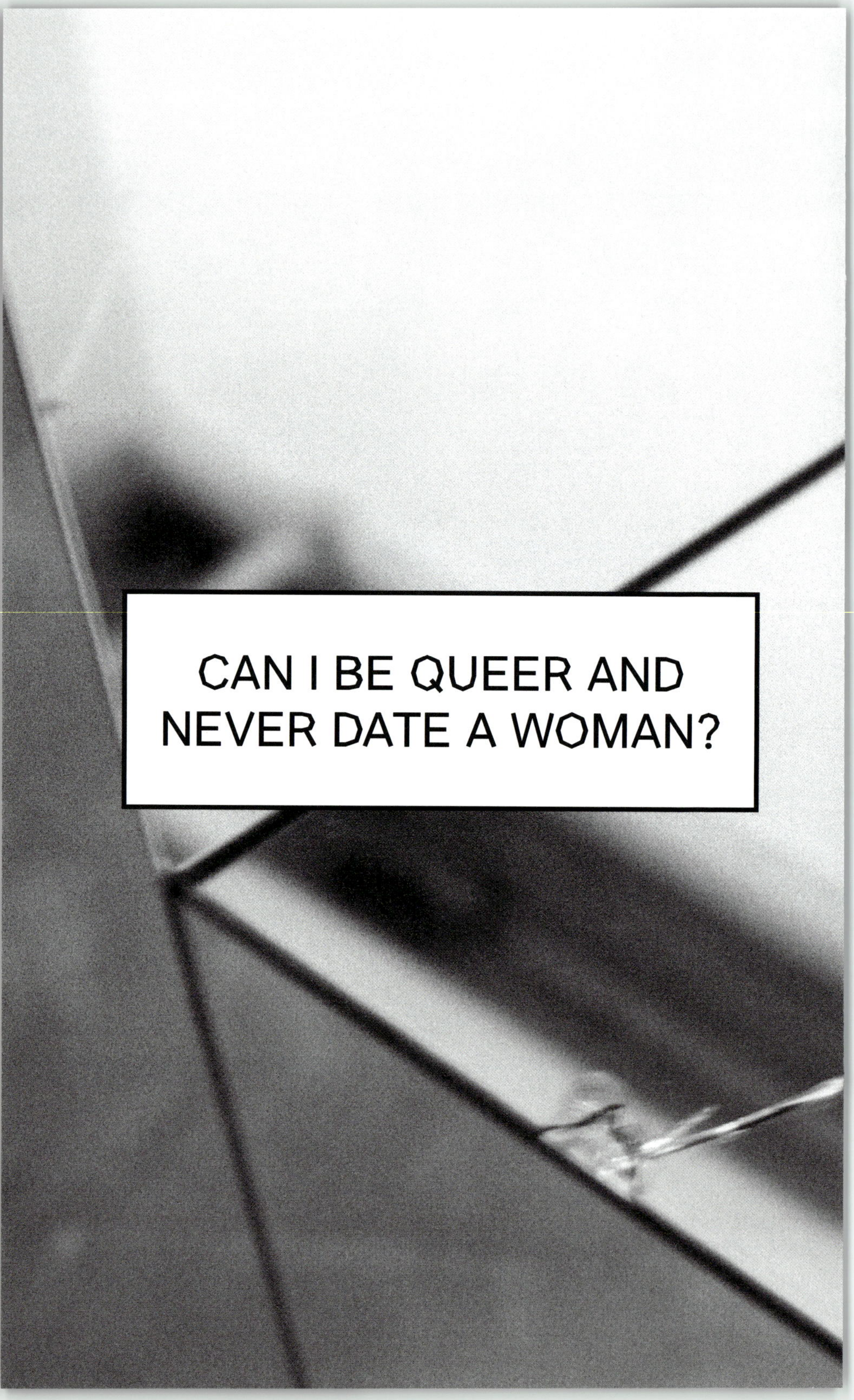

CAN I BE QUEER AND NEVER DATE A WOMAN?

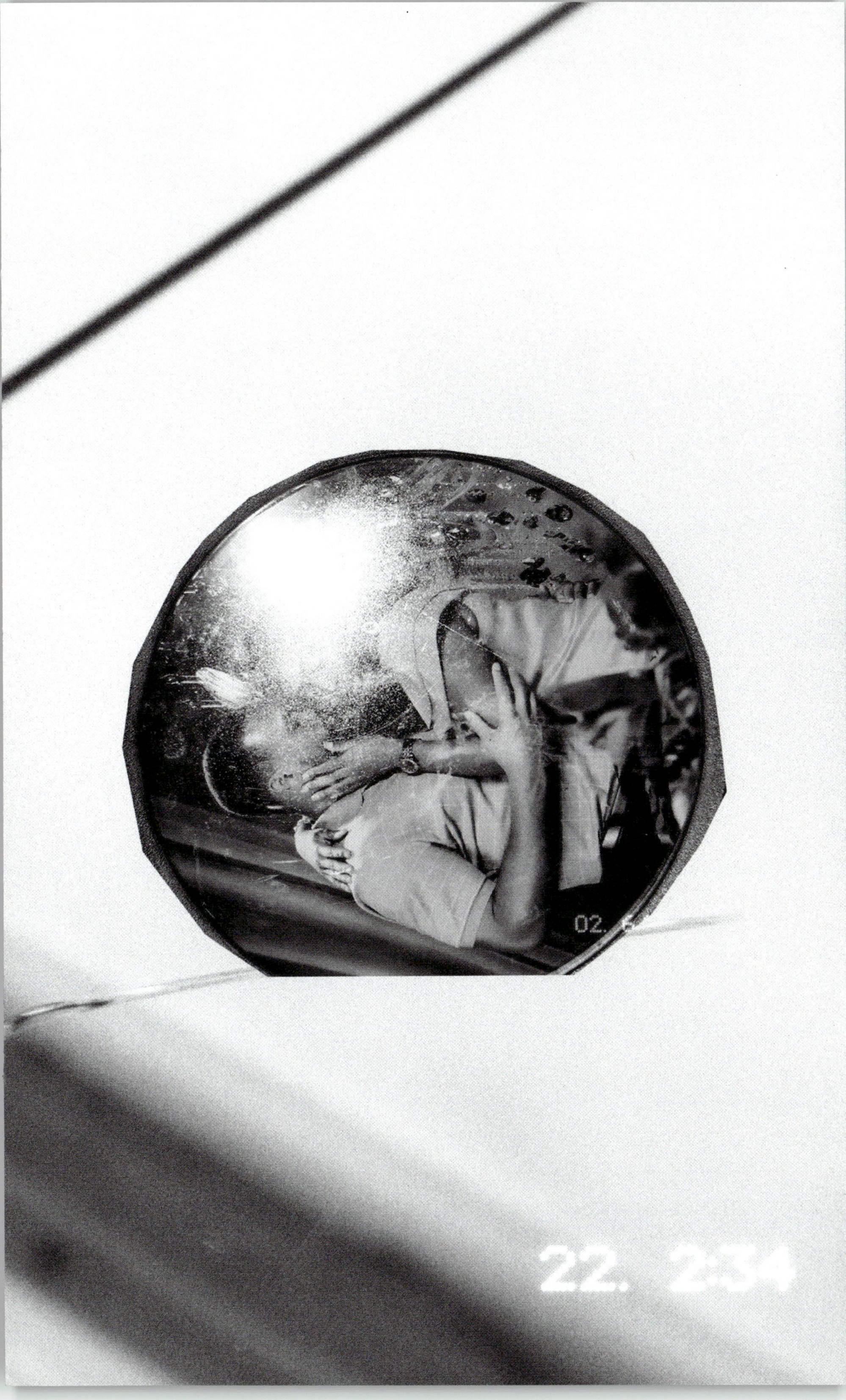
02.
22. 2:34

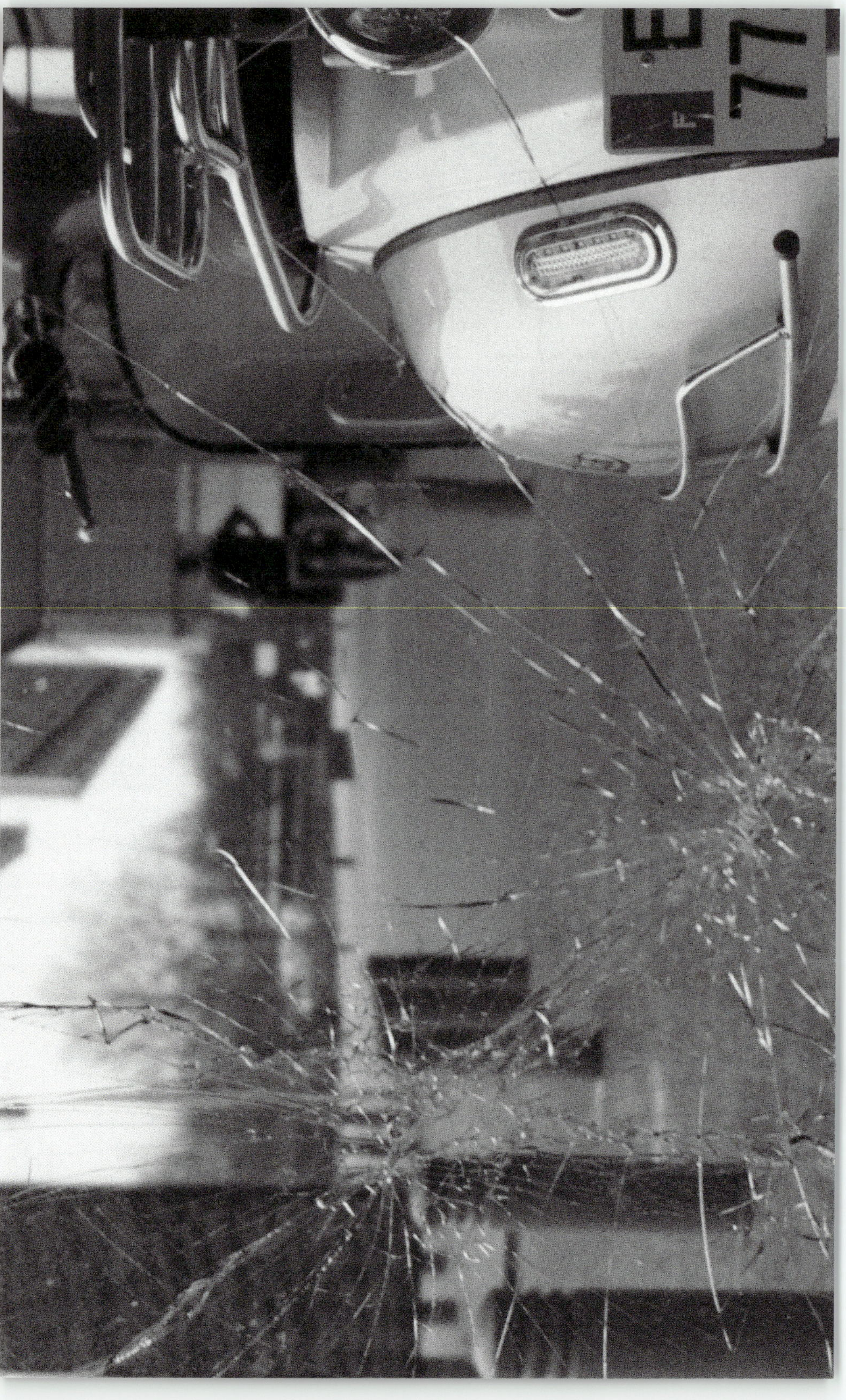

Societal call 2

t to wa

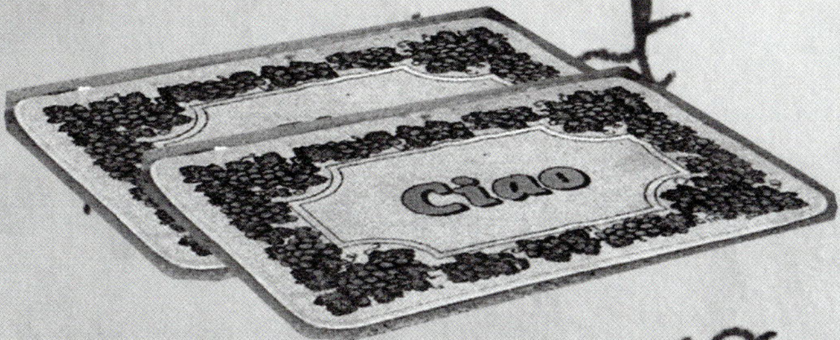

God venus ven

---

ct 6th 6:01 am ~~morning~~ f

KILL ALL MEN! K

~~[illegible]~~ I hate the

selfish, small-minded

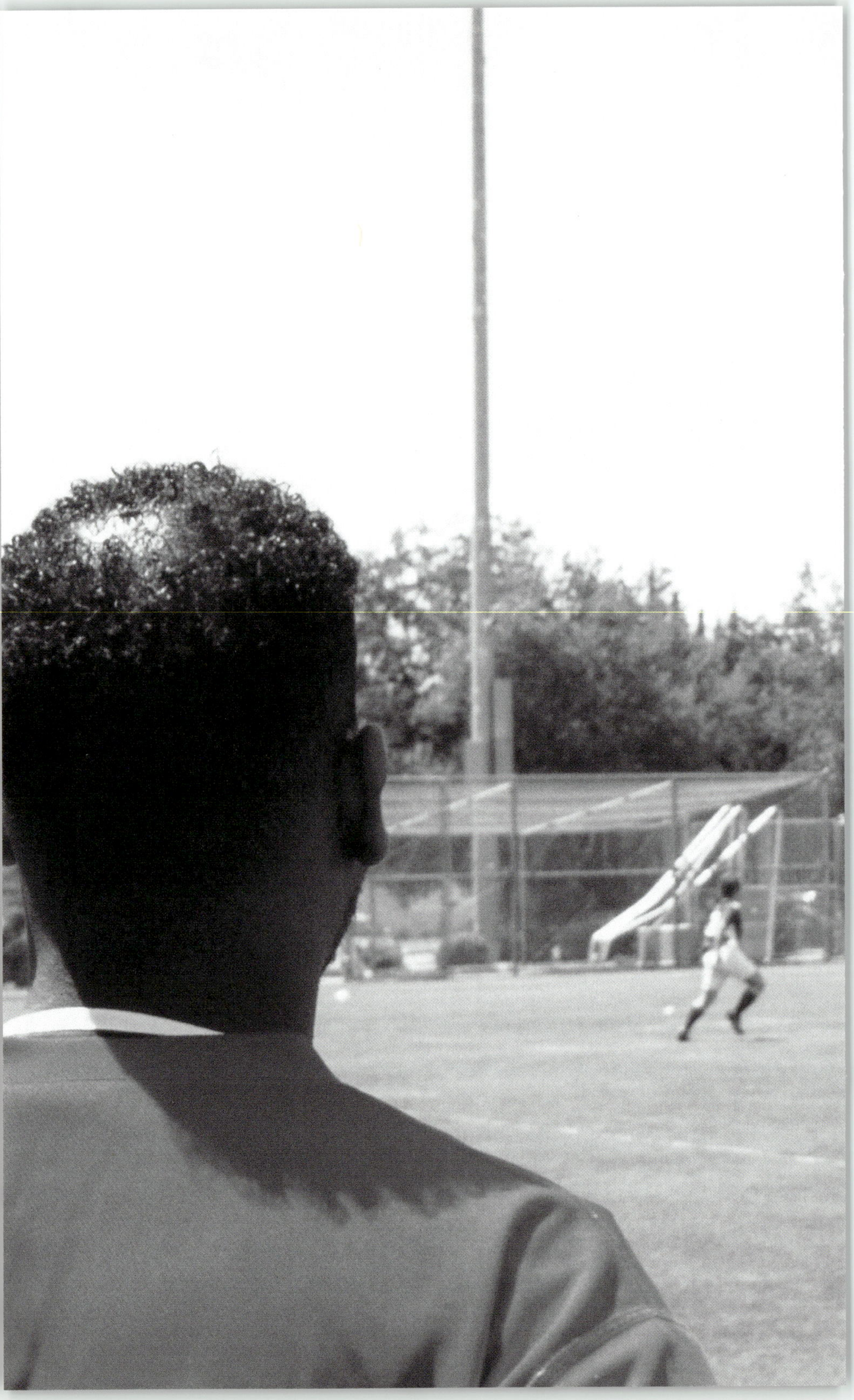

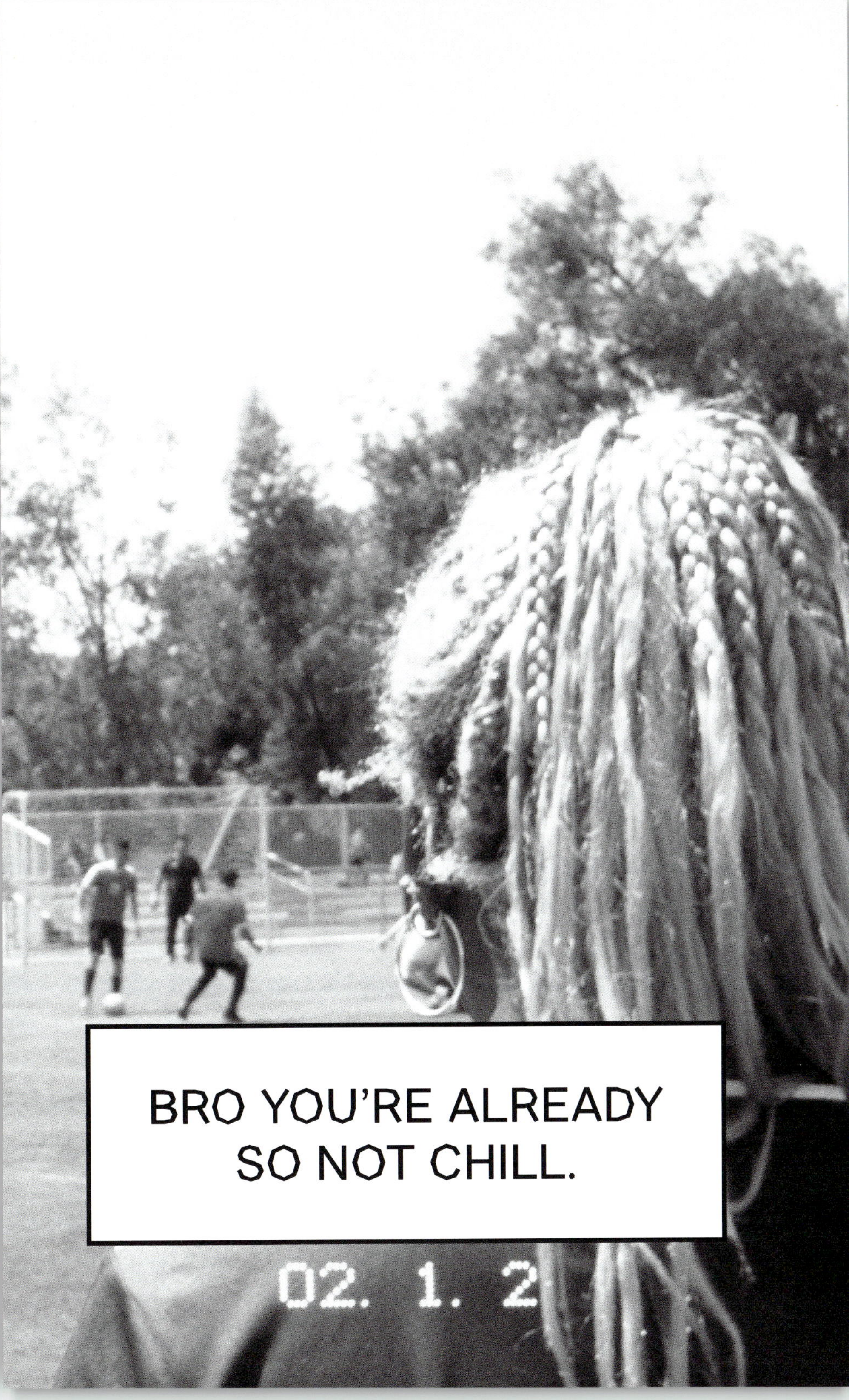
BRO YOU'RE ALREADY
SO NOT CHILL.
02. 1. 2

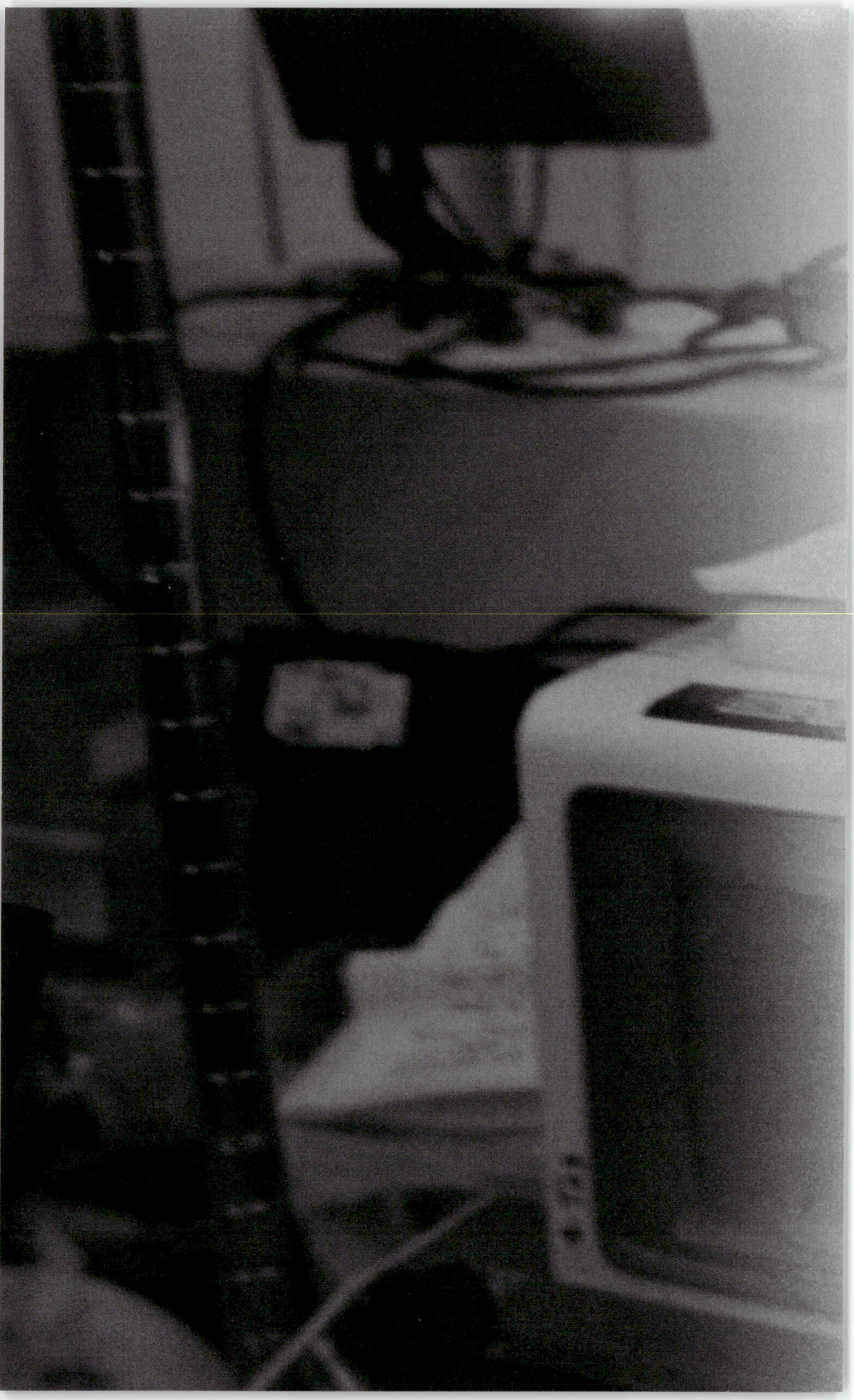

PEELING MY TOE
NAIL OFF, PLUCKING
HAIRS OUT OF MY
SKIN, WAXING, THE
DENTISTS, BITING,
PUNCHING, ROUGH,
HARD SEX, HAVING MY
ASS SLAPPED, HAVING
MY BODY SQUEEZED

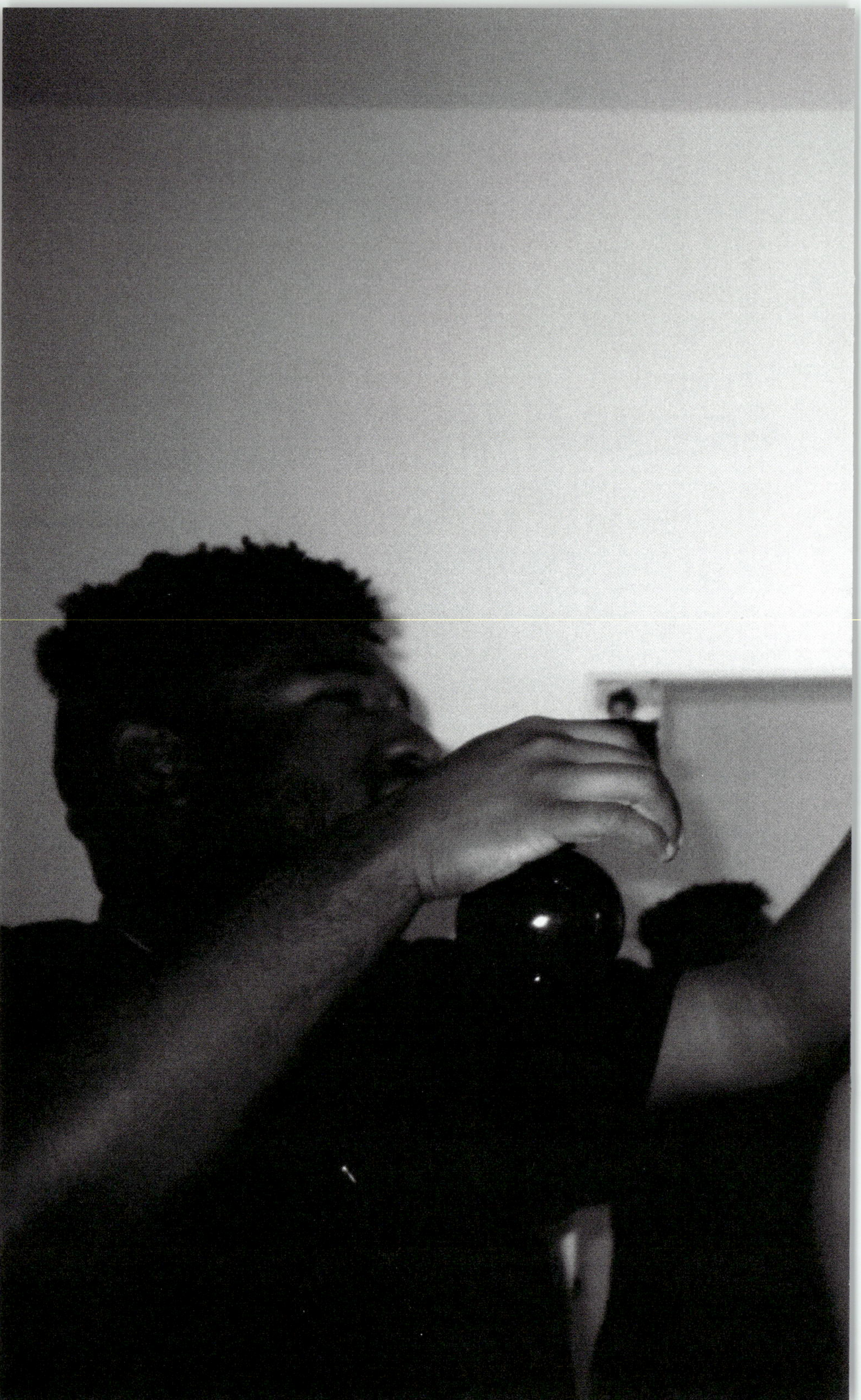

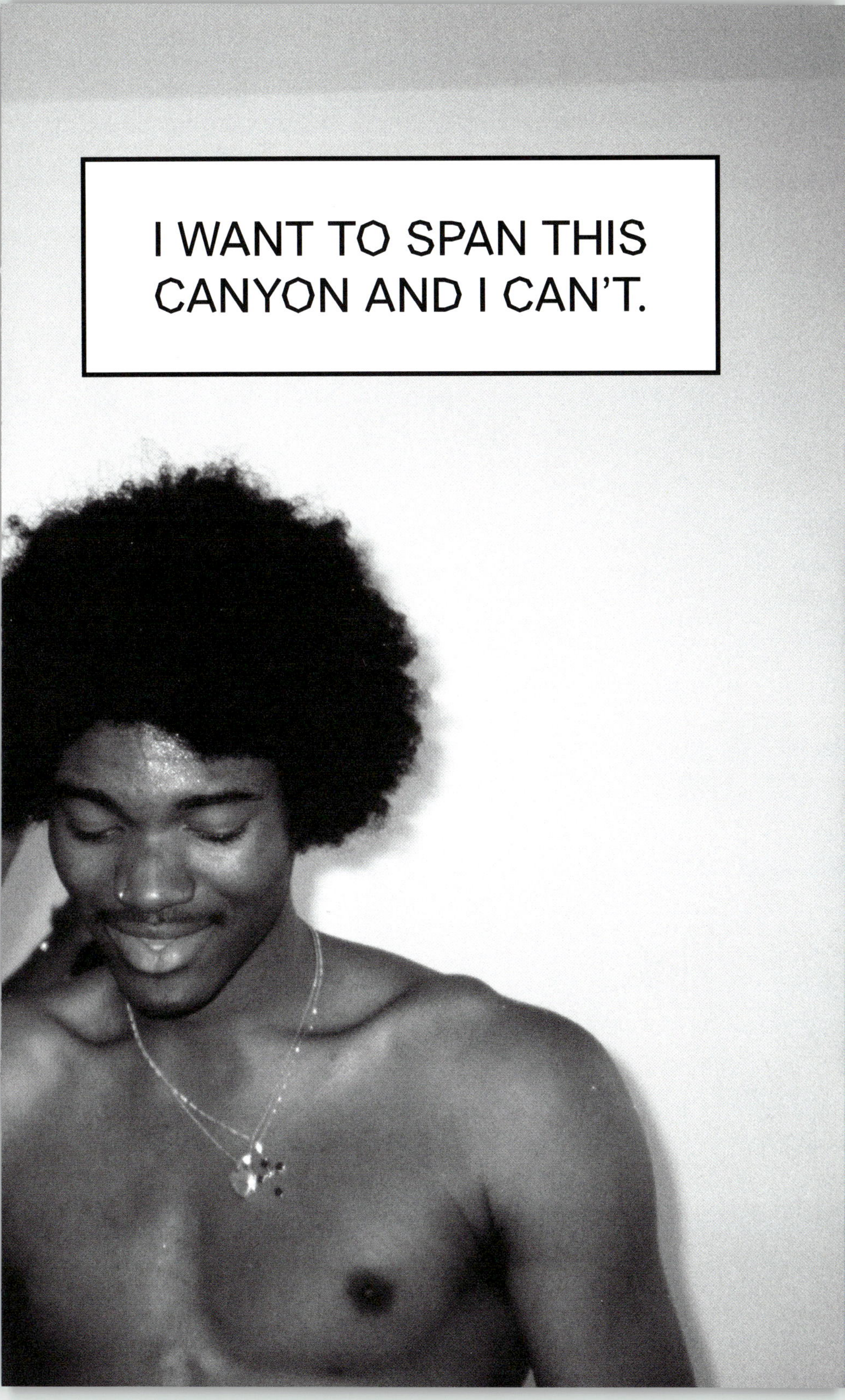
I WANT TO SPAN THIS
CANYON AND I CAN'T.

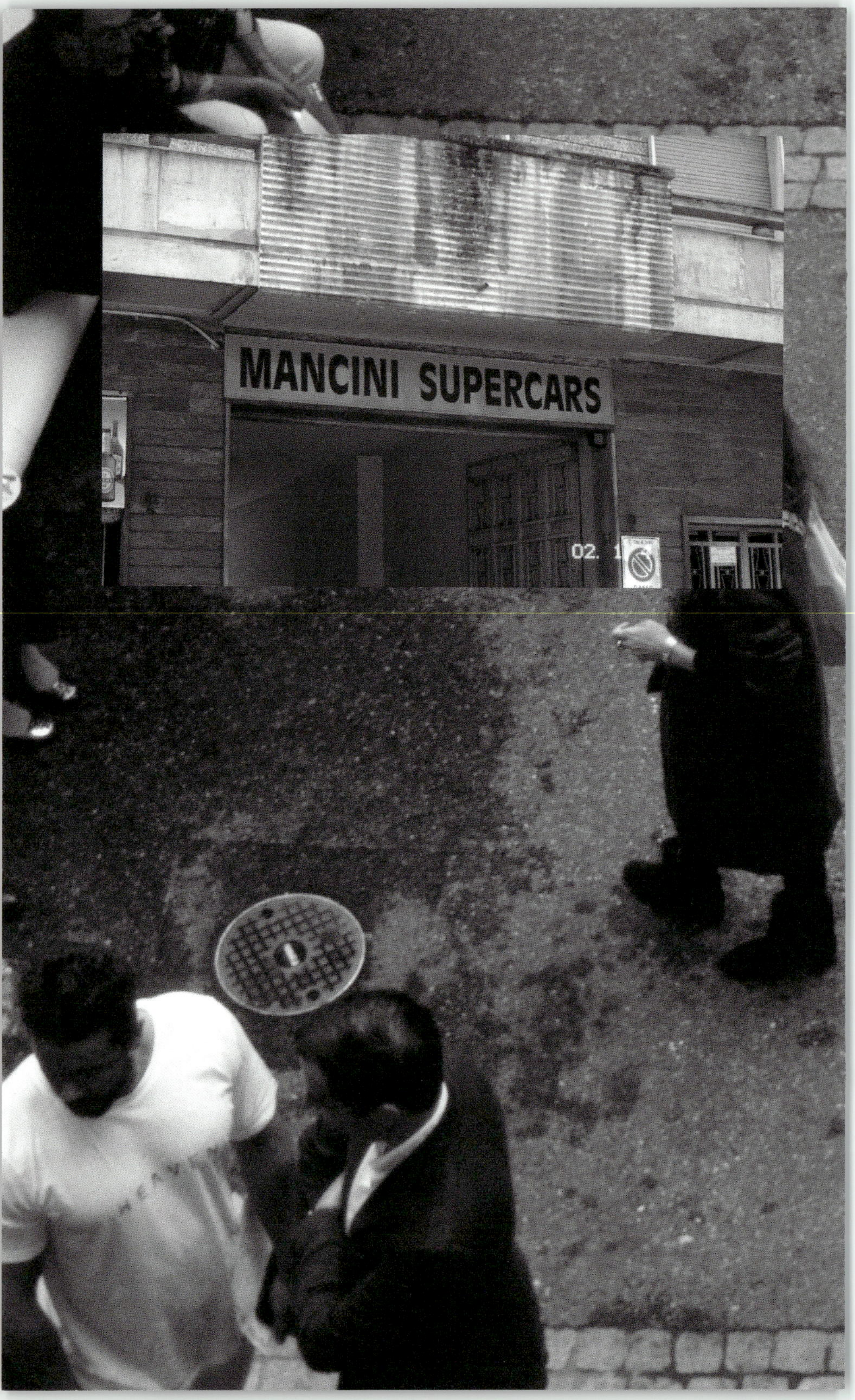
MANCINI SUPERCARS

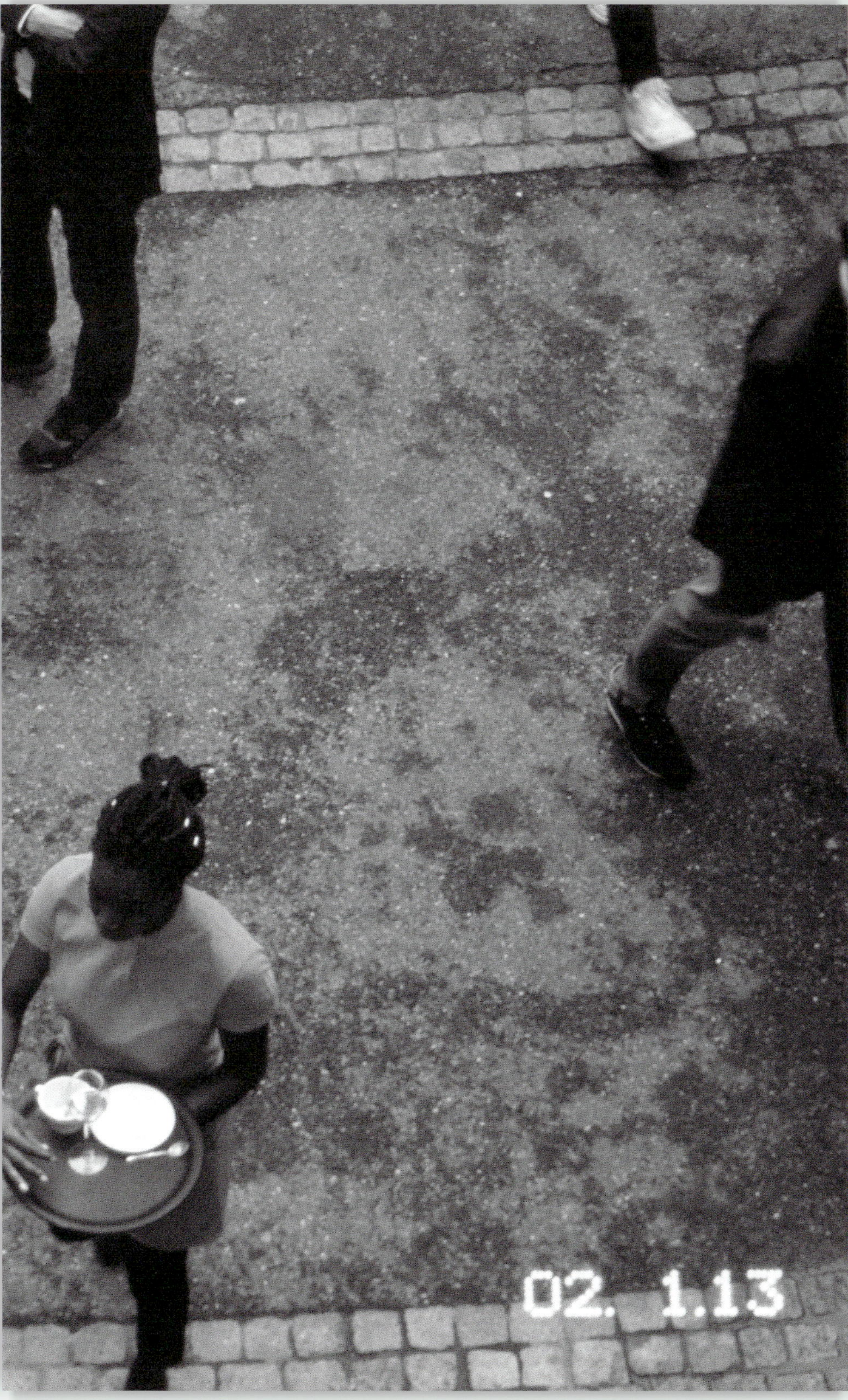
02. 1.13

I LIKE TO BE DOMMED IN THE BEDROOM NOT LIFE!

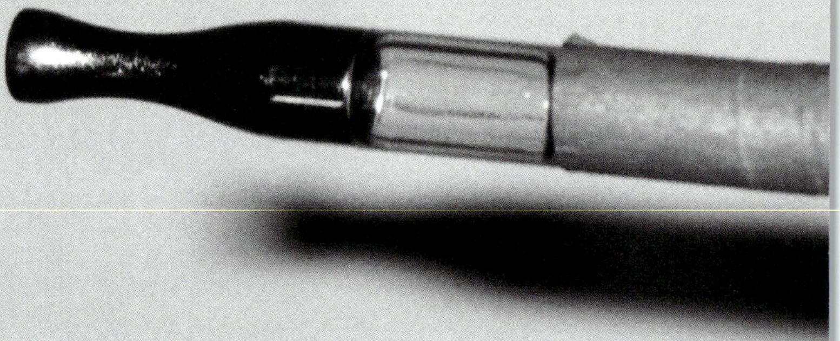

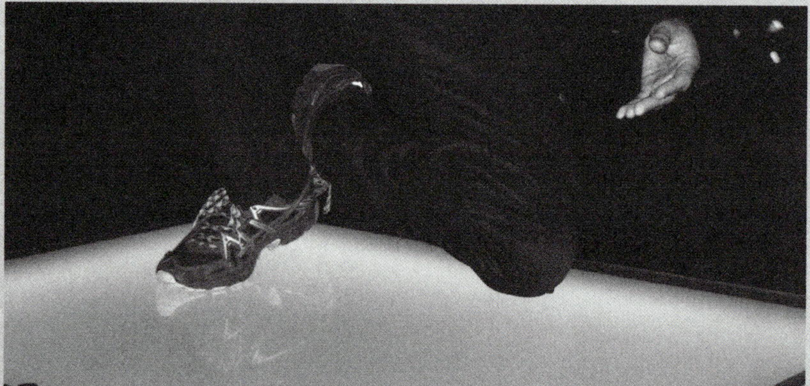

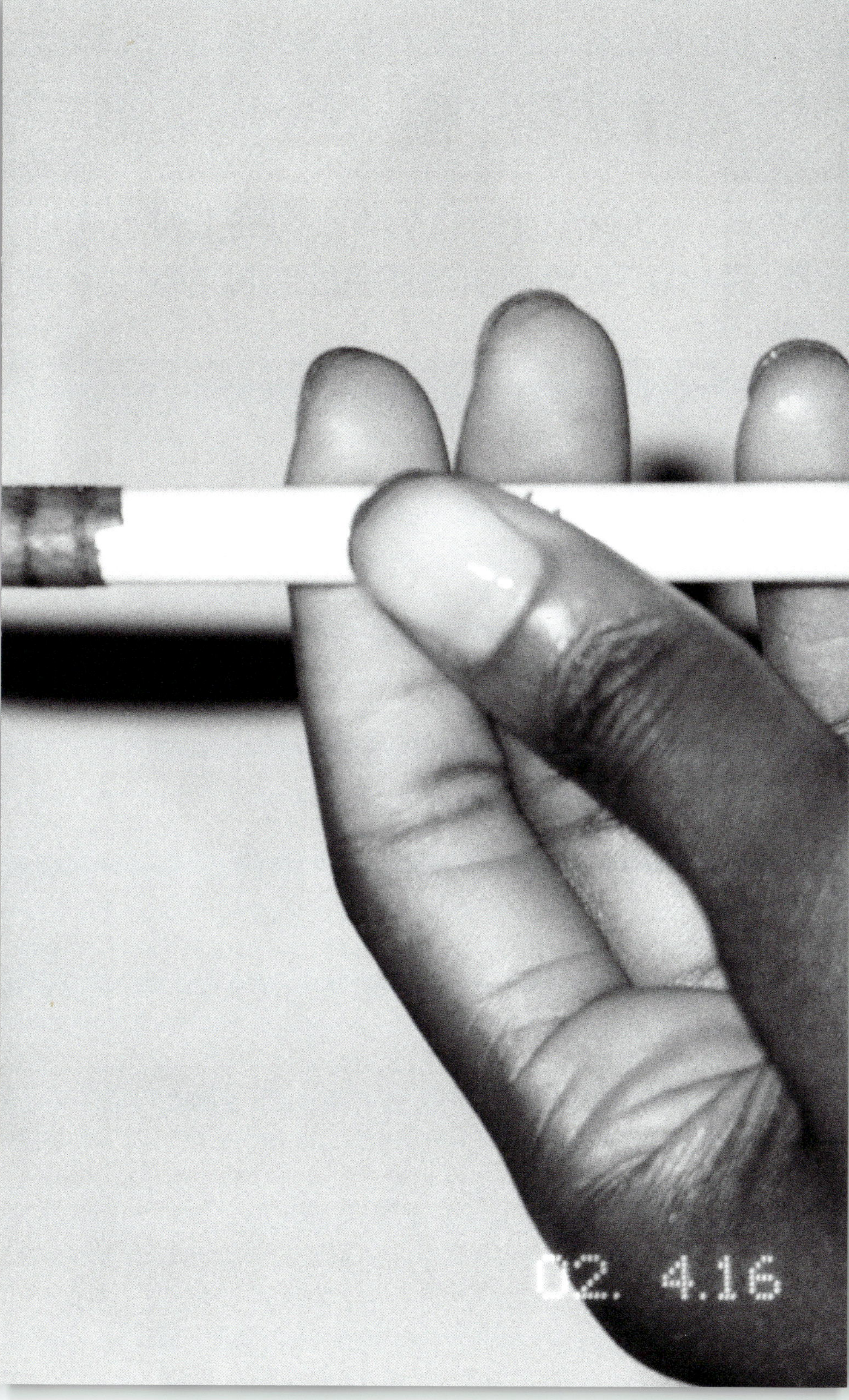
02. 4.16

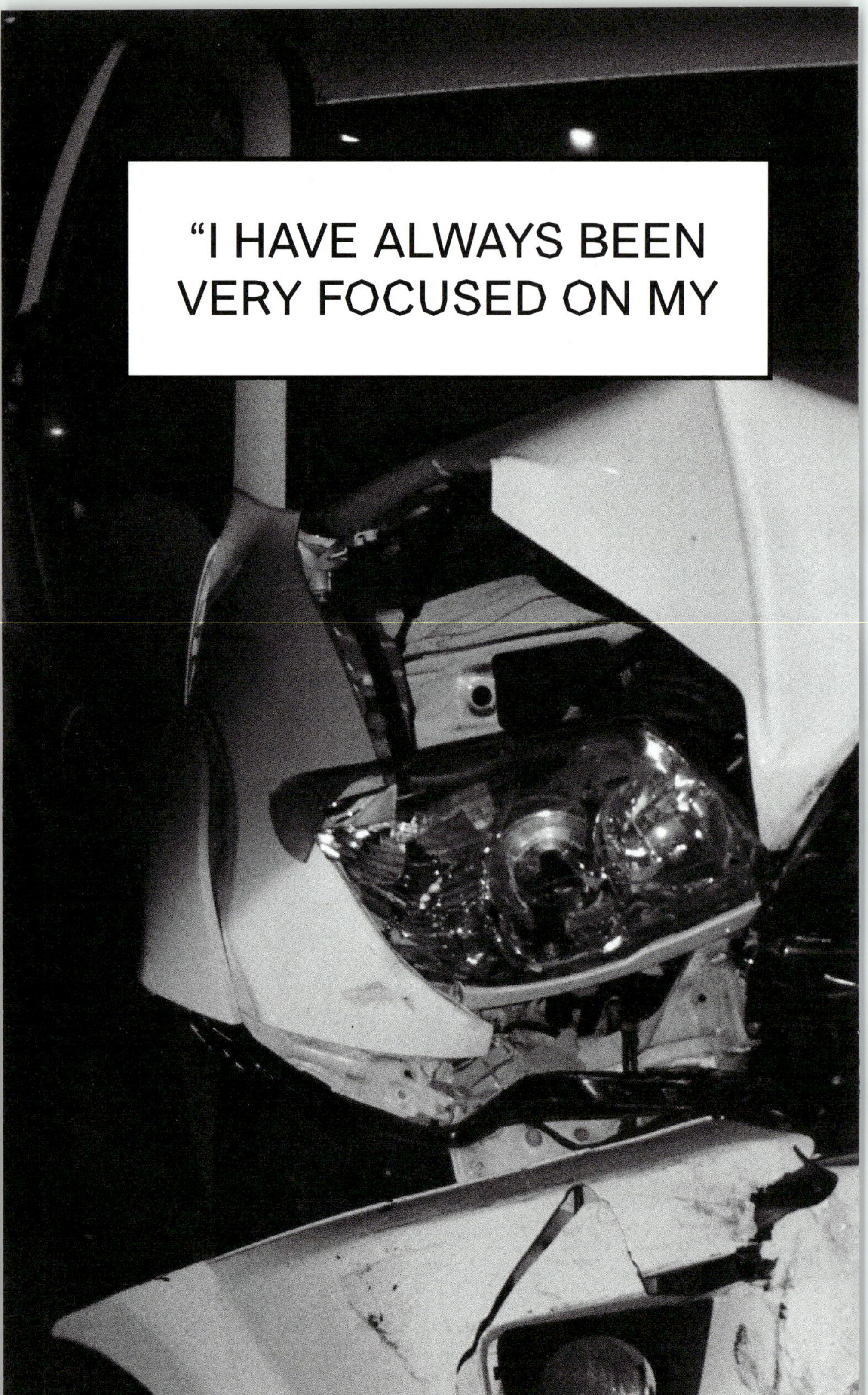
"I HAVE ALWAYS BEEN
VERY FOCUSED ON MY

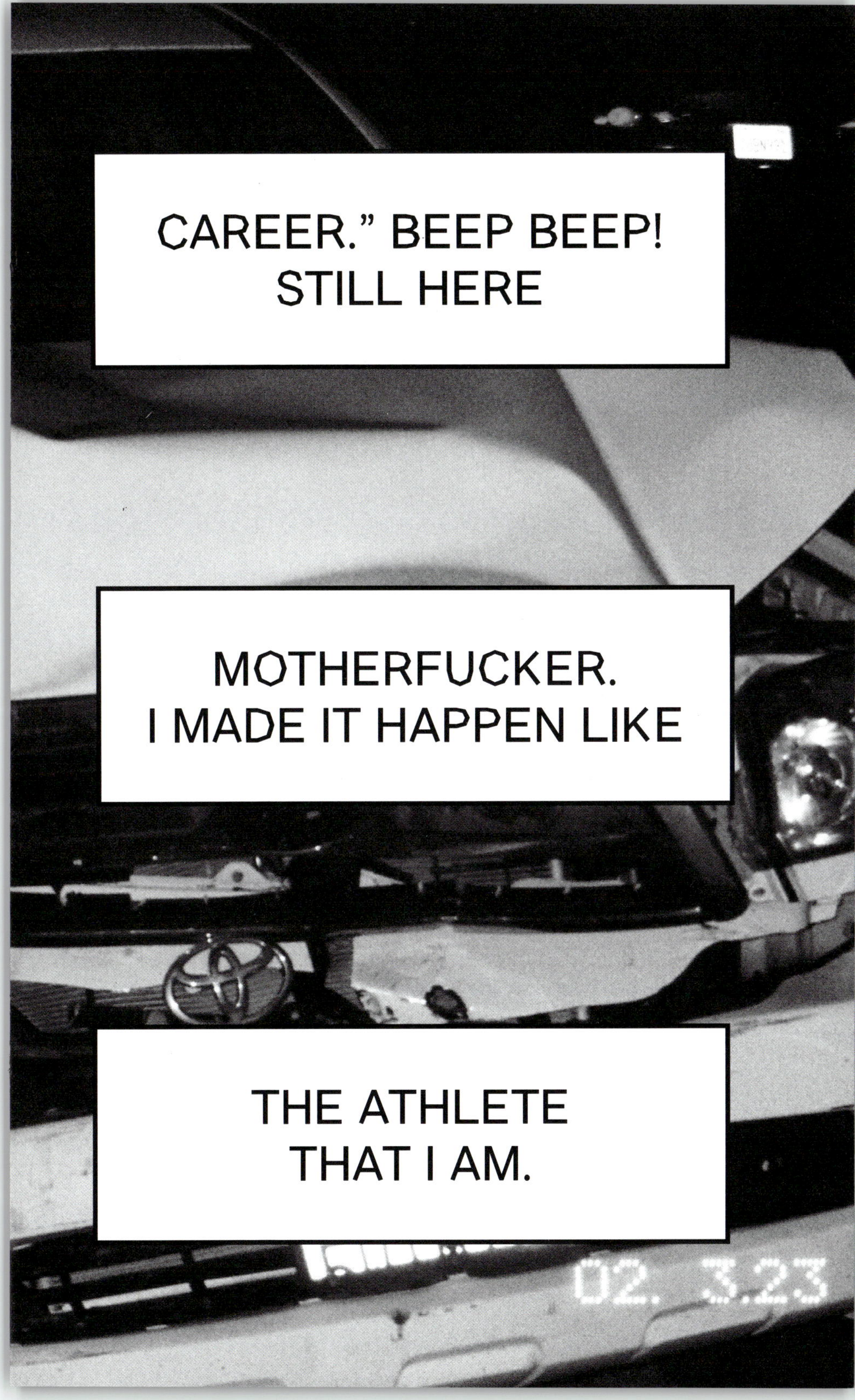
CAREER." BEEP BEEP! STILL HERE
MOTHERFUCKER. I MADE IT HAPPEN LIKE
THE ATHLETE THAT I AM.
02. 3.23